W9-CVY-112

WordPerfect 5.1

Timothy J. O'Leary
Linda I. O'Leary

REVISED
NEW PROBLEMS
AND
PRACTICE
EXERCISES

4 5 6 7 8 9 0 BAN BAN 9 0 9 8 7 6 5 4

ISBN 0-07-048896-7

Library of Congress Catalog Card Number 93-78733

CONTENTS

Word Processing

The most popular applications software used on a microcomputer today is a word processor. To put your thoughts in writing, from the simplest note to the most complex book, is a time-consuming process. Even more time-consuming is the task of editing and retyping the document to make it perfect. There was a time that perfection in written communication was difficult, if not impossible, to achieve. With the introduction of word processing, errors should be nearly nonexistent—not because they are not made, but because they are easy to correct. Word processors let you throw away the correction fluid, scissors, paste, and erasers. Now, with a few keystrokes, you can correct errors, move paragraphs, and reprint your document easily.

Definition of Word Processing

Word processing applications software is a program that helps you create any type of written communication via a keyboard. A word processor can be used to manipulate text data to produce a letter, a report, a memo, or any other type of correspondence. Text data is any letter, number, or symbol that you can type on a keyboard. The grouping of the text data to form words, sentences, paragraphs, and pages of text results in the creation of a document. Through a word processor you can create, modify, store, retrieve, and print part or all of a document.

Advantages of Using a Word Processor

The speed of entering text data into the computer depends on the skill of the user. If you cannot type fast, a word processor will not improve your typing speed. However, a word processor will make it easier to correct and change your document. Consequently, your completed document will take less time to create.

Where a word processor excels is in its ability to change, modify, or edit a document. Editing involves correcting spelling, grammar, and sentence-structure errors. With a word processor, the text is stored on the diskette. As errors are found, they are electronically deleted and corrected. Once the document is the way you want it to appear, it is printed on paper. Goodbye, correction fluid!

In addition to editing a document, you can easily revise or update it through the insertion or deletion of text. For example, a document that lists prices can easily be updated to reflect new prices. A document that details procedures can be revised by deleting old procedures and inserting new ones. This is especially helpful when a document is used repeatedly. Rather than recreating the whole document, only the parts that change need to be revised.

Revision also includes the rearrangement of pieces or blocks of text. For example, while writing a report, you may decide to change the location of a single word or several paragraphs or pages of text. You can do it easily by using Block and Move commands. Blocks of text can also be copied from one area of the document to another. This is a real advantage when the text includes many recurring phrases or words.

Combining text in another file with your document is another advantage of word processors. An example of this is a group term paper. Each person is responsible for writing a section of the paper. Before printing the document, the text for all sections, which is stored in different files, is combined to create the complete paper. The opposite is also true. Text that may not be appropriate in your document can easily be put in another file for later use.

Many word processors include special programs to further help you produce a perfect document. A spell checker will check the spelling in a document by comparing each word to a dictionary of words. If an error is found, the program will suggest the correct spelling. A syntax checker electronically checks grammar, phrasing, capitalization, and other types of syntax errors in a document. A thesaurus will display different words, each with a meaning similar to the word you entered.

After changes are made and the document appears ready to be printed, the word processor also makes it easy to change the design or appearance of the document. For example, a word processor lets you set the line spacing of a document. You can decide how large you want the right, left, top, and bottom margins. The number of lines printed on each page can be specified. In addition, you can quickly specify whether the pages will or will not be numbered and where (top or bottom, centered or not) the number will appear. Further, a word processor will let you enter headers and footers on each page or specified pages.

If, after reading the printed copy, you find other errors or want to revise or reformat the document, it is easy to do. Simply reload the document file, make your changes, and reprint the text! Now that saves time!

Word Processing Terminology

The following list of terms and definitions are generic in nature and are associated with most word processing programs.

Block: Any group of characters, words, lines, paragraphs, or pages of text.

Boldface: Produces dark or heavy print.

Center: Centers a line of text evenly between the margins.

Character string: Any combination of letters, numbers, symbols, and spaces.

Delete: To erase a character, word, paragraph, or block of text from the document.

Flush right: Aligns text on the right-hand margin.

Format: Defines how the printed document will appear; includes settings for underline, boldface, print size, margin settings, line spacing, etc.

Insert mode: Allows new text to be entered into a document between existing text.

Justified: The text has even left and right margins, produced by inserting extra spaces between words on each line.

Merge: Combine text in one document with text in another.

Overstrike: Causes the printer to print one character over another to make the type darker.

Search: Scans the document for all matching character strings.

Search and replace: Scans the document for all matching character strings and replaces them with others.

Template: A document, like a form letter, that contains blank spaces for automatic insertion of information that varies from one document to another.

Typeover mode: New text is entered in a document by typing over the existing text on the line.

Unjustified: The text has an even left margin and an uneven, or ragged, right margin.

Word wrap: Automatic adjustment of number of characters or words on a line while entering text; eliminates pressing the ⏎ (Return) key at the end of each line.

Case Study for Labs 1- 4

Karen Barnes is the membership assistant for the Sports Club. The club just purchased a word processing program. Her first assignment using the software package is to create a letter welcoming new members to the club.

In Lab 1, the rough draft of the letter entered by Karen is corrected. During this process, the basic cursor-movement keys and editing features are demonstrated.

Lab 2 continues with modifying the welcome letter by entering new text, combining files, and rearranging paragraphs and blocks of text. The print, line, and page formats are modified, and the completed document is printed.

In Lab 3, the welcome letter is changed to a form letter using the Merge feature. Next, another document is created using text taken from the welcome letter. The Split Screen feature lets the user view both documents on the screen at the same time, greatly simplifying the process. Finally, the document is changed to column format to be used in the club newsletter.

In the final word processing lab, Peg, a student intern at the Sports Club, is writing a term paper. As part of this process you will learn how to create an outline, produce a table of contents, and enter footnotes. Several new format features are also demonstrated.

Editing a Document

1

OBJECTIVES

In this lab you will learn how to:

1. Load the WordPerfect 5.1 program.
2. Issue a WordPerfect 5.1 command.
3. Retrieve a file.
4. Move around a document.
5. Delete characters, words, and lines of text.
6. Undelete text.
7. Insert text in Insert and Typeover modes.
8. Insert and delete blank lines.
9. Clear the display.
10. List file names.
11. Save and replace a file.
12. Print a document.
13. Exit WordPerfect 5.1.

CASE STUDY

Karen Barnes, the membership assistant for the Sports Club, has been asked to create a letter welcoming new members to the club. The letter should briefly explain the services offered by the club. Karen has written a rough draft of the welcome letter using WordPerfect 5.1. However, it contains many errors. You will follow Karen as she uses WordPerfect 5.1 to correct and modify the letter.

Loading the WordPerfect 5.1 Program

Starting WordPerfect on a Two-Disk System

Boot the system by turning on the computer and loading DOS. After you have responded to the DOS date and time prompts, the A> should appear on your display screen.

Remove the DOS diskette and place the backup WordPerfect 1 diskette in the A drive and the backup data diskette in the B drive.

To load the WordPerfect 5.1 program, you will begin by changing the default disk drive to B. This tells the system that the diskette in the B drive will be used to save and retrieve files. At the A>,

Type: B:
Press: ⏎

To tell the system that the WordPerfect program diskette is in the A drive and to load the program into memory,

Type: A:WP
Press: ⏎

After a few moments, your display screen should provide copyright information, the version number of your copy, and the default drive that the system will use.

This screen also prompts you to insert the WordPerfect 2 disk. Follow these directions by removing the WordPerfect 1 disk from drive A, inserting the WordPerfect 2 disk, and pressing any key.

The editing screen is displayed. Skip to the section, "The Editing Screen," on the next page.

Starting WordPerfect on a Hard-Disk System

The WordPerfect program should have already been installed on your hard disk. It is assumed that the program files are on the C drive in the subdirectory \WP. If yours is in a different drive or subdirectory, substitute the appropriate drive and subdirectory name in the directions below.

The drive door(s) should be open. Turn on your computer and, if necessary, respond to the date and time prompts. The DOS C> should be displayed.

Put your data disk in drive A and, if necessary, close the door.

To load the WordPerfect 5.1 program, begin by changing the default disk drive to A. At the C>,

Type: A:
Press: ⏎

Drive A is now the default drive. This means that the diskette in the A drive will be used to save and retrieve files. Now you are ready to load the WordPerfect program. The command, WP, will load the program into memory. You must include the drive and subdirectory path as part of the command to tell the system where to find the WordPerfect files. To do this,

Type: C:\WP\WP
Press: ⏎

After a few moments, your screen should briefly display the opening screen. This screen contains copyright information, the version number of your copy, and the default drive that the system will use. This is quickly replaced with the Editing screen.

WORD PROCESSING

The Editing Screen

Your display screen should be similar to Figure 1-1.

FIGURE 1-1

This is a blank WordPerfect 5.1 Editing screen. The blinking line or dash in the upper left corner is the **cursor**. It shows you where the next character you type will appear.

The line of information at the bottom of the screen is the **status line**. It displays four items of information about the current location of the cursor:

Doc 1   This shows which **document** window displays the cursor. A **window** is an area of the screen which displays the document. You can enter and edit text in two separate windows at a time. These windows are displayed as Doc 1 or Doc 2 in the status line. Currently, the cursor is in the document 1 window, and the window occupies the entire screen.

Pg 1   This shows the number of the **page** the cursor is located on. A page refers to the physical page when a document is printed. It is currently on page 1.

Ln 1"   This tells you the vertical distance in inches between the cursor and the top of the page. This is the **line** on which the cursor rests. The cursor is currently 1 inch from the top of the page.

Pos 1"   This tells you the horizontal location, or **position** of the cursor on the line. The position is displayed in inches from the left edge of the page. The cursor is currently 1 inch from the left edge of the page.

The line and position locations of the cursor you see on your screen are **default,** or initial, WordPerfect 5.1 settings. WordPerfect comes with many default settings. These are generally the most commonly used settings. For example, the current position of the cursor at 1 inch from the left edge of the page is the default left margin setting. The right margin default setting is 1 inch from the right edge of the page. When the document is printed, the printed page will have 1-inch left and right margins. Other default settings include a standard paper-size setting of 8-1/2 by 11 inches, tab settings every .5 inch, and single line spacing. If you do not specify different settings, WordPerfect uses the default settings.

Entering WordPerfect 5.1 Commands

The WordPerfect 5.1 editing screen is blank, except for the status line. Commands are entered using the pull-down menus or the function keys. Both methods produce the same result.

Using the Pull-Down Menu

A **pull-down menu** displays a list of commands in a box that are available for selection when the menu is selected. Using the pull-down menu lets you see the various commands and options available. This is particularly helpful to people who are just learning to use the program.

To activate the pull-down menu,

Press: (ALT) - = (hold down (ALT) while pressing =)

Your display screen should be similar to Figure 1-2.

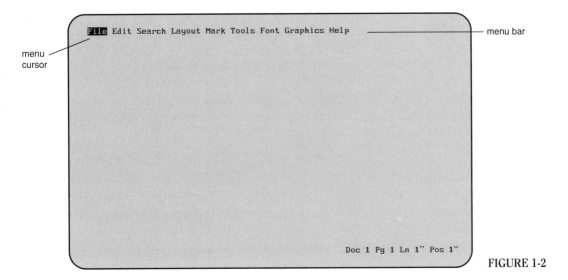

FIGURE 1-2

The top line of the screen displays the **menu bar**. It lists the names of nine menus which can be opened. The first menu name, File, is highlighted with the **menu cursor**. The (→) and (←) keys are used to move the menu cursor in the direction of the arrow from one menu name to the next.

Press: (→)

The menu cursor is positioned on Edit.

Press: (→) (8 times)

The menu cursor has moved to each menu name and in a circular fashion has returned to the File menu.

To activate the pull-down menu of commands associated with the highlighted menu,

Press: ⟵┘

Your display screen should be similar to Figure 1-3.

FIGURE 1-3

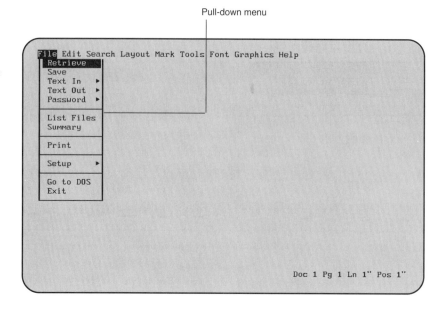

Pull-down menu

The pull-down menu of commands is displayed in a box below the File menu name, and the first pull-down menu command, Retrieve, is highlighted.

Note: Newer releases of WordPerfect 5.1 show function key command equivalents in the menus.

Now pressing → will move the menu cursor to the next pull-down menu.

Press: →

The Edit pull-down menu is displayed. Notice that the menu cursor is not positioned on the first command, Move; instead it is positioned on the third command, Paste. This is because the first two commands are not available for selection at this time. Pull-down menu commands which cannot be selected are surrounded by brackets ([]). Additionally the menu cursor cannot be positioned on a command that is not available for selection.

The ↑ and ↓ keys are used to move the menu cursor within the pull-down menu.

Press: ↓

The menu cursor has moved to the next available command, Undelete.

Press: ↓ (2 times)

Your display screen should be similar to Figure 1-4.

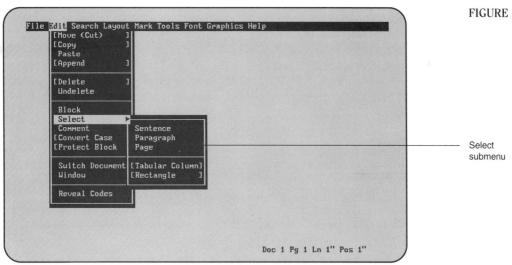

Select
submenu

The menu cursor is positioned on Select. Notice the > symbol following the command name. This symbol tells you that a **submenu** of options will be displayed when the command is highlighted. In this case, the submenu consists of the options displayed in the box to the right.

Press: $\rightarrow$

The menu cursor remains positioned on the pull-down command, Select, and another menu cursor highlights the first submenu option, Sentence. The $\uparrow$ and $\downarrow$ keys are used to move around the submenu.

Press: $\downarrow$

The submenu cursor is positioned on Paragraph.

Press: $\leftarrow$

The submenu cursor is cleared.

Press: (PGDN)

The menu cursor is positioned on the last command in the Edit menu, Reveal Codes. Pressing (PGDN) or (PGUP) in a pull-down menu or submenu will quickly move the menu cursor to the first or last command in the menu.

Press: (PGUP)

The menu cursor is positioned back on Paste. To see what commands are available in the other menus,

Press: $\rightarrow$ (9 times)

The File pull-down menu should be displayed. To remove the pull-down menu,

Press: (ESC)

Pressing (ESC) when a menu is displayed "backs up," or cancels, the previous selection.

When a pull-down menu is not displayed a quick way to move the menu cursor to the last menu name in the menu bar from any location on the bar is to press (END).

Press: (END)

The menu cursor is positioned on Help. The same action could have been accomplished using (HOME), (→); however, it requires an extra keystroke.

Press: (←)

The menu cursor moved one menu to the left. To move quickly to the first menu, File,

Press: (HOME) , (←)

A quicker way to move to and activate a pull-down menu is to type the **mnemonic letter** (the highlighted letter associated with the menu name) of the menu you want to select. To select **H**elp,

Type: **H**

The Help menu is selected, and the pull-down menu of commands is displayed.

So far you have moved the menu cursor to highlight many commands. However, you have not yet selected or executed a command. A command is selected by highlighting the command with the menu cursor and pressing (⏎) , or by typing the mnemonic letter associated with the command.

Note: If you find that you have selected the wrong command, use Cancel ((F1)) to cancel the selection, or (ESC) to back out of a selected menu.

The menu cursor is over the first command, Help. Since this command is highlighted, it can be selected by pressing (⏎) . It can also be selected by typing the mnemonic letter "h."

Select: Help

Your display screen should be similar to Figure 1-5.

FIGURE 1-5

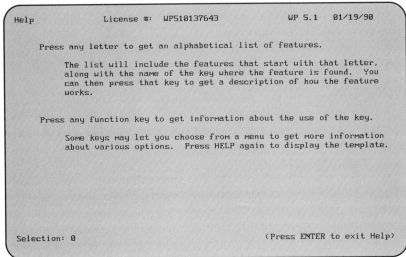

```
Help                License #:  WP510137643          WP 5.1   01/19/90


     Press any letter to get an alphabetical list of features.

        The list will include the features that start with that letter,
        along with the name of the key where the feature is found.  You
        can then press that key to get a description of how the feature
        works.


     Press any function key to get information about the use of the key.

        Some keys may let you choose from a menu to get more information
        about various options.  Press HELP again to display the template.










  Selection: 0                          (Press ENTER to exit Help)
```

You have executed the Help menu's Help command. A full screen of information about how the Help system works is displayed. You will use Help shortly for more information. For now, following the directions on the screen to exit Help,

Press: ⏎

You are returned to the blank Editing screen. Once a command is executed and completed, you are returned to the Editing screen rather than to the menu.

Using a Mouse

If you have a mouse attached to your computer, follow the instructions below. If you do not have a mouse, skip to the next section, "Using the Function Keys."

The mouse controls a pointer on your screen. As soon as you move the mouse the pointer appears.

Move the mouse in any direction.

The pointer appears as a solid rectangle. You move the pointer on the screen by moving the mouse over the desk top in the direction you want the pointer to move.

Move the mouse in all directions (up, down, left, and right) and note the movement of the pointer on the screen.

If you pick up the mouse and move it to a different location on your desk top, the pointer will not move on the screen. This is because the pointer movement is controlled by the rubber-coated ball on the bottom of the mouse. This ball must move within its socket in order for the pointer to move on the screen. The ball's movement is translated into signals that tell the computer how to move the on-screen pointer.

On top of the mouse are two or three buttons. These buttons are used to enter user input instructions. Quickly pressing and releasing a mouse button is called clicking. To activate the WordPerfect 5.1 menu bar, click the right mouse button.

The menu bar appears at the top of the screen, just as if you had used the keyboard equivalent, (ALT) - =. (See Figure 1-2.)

Move the mouse so that the pointer is within the menu bar.

Move the mouse to the right and left to move the pointer from one menu name to the next. This has the same effect as using the $\rightarrow$ and $\leftarrow$ keys to move the menu cursor within the menu bar.

Position the pointer anywhere within File on the menu bar. To activate the pull-down menu,

Click: Left button

Note: If the pointer is not on a menu name when you click the left button, the menu will be cleared from the screen. If this happens, click the right button again to display the menu bar and try again.

The pull-down menu of commands is displayed below the File menu name, and the menu cursor is positioned on Retrieve. This is the same as if you had pressed $\leftarrow\!\!\lrcorner$ using the keyboard (See Figure 1-3).

With the pointer still in the menu bar, hold down the left mouse button and move the mouse slowly to the right along the menu bar. Do not release the left button until the pointer is positioned over Tools.

Note: If, when you release the left button, the pointer is not on a menu name, the menu bar is cleared from the screen. If this happens, click the right button again to re-display the menu bar and try again.

Note: Developing the skill for moving the mouse and correctly positioning the pointer takes some time. If you accidentally find yourself in the wrong location or in a command that you did not intend to select, click the right button on a two-button mouse or the center button on a three-button mouse. This action will cancel most selected commands.

The process of holding down the left button as you move the mouse is called **dragging**. After dragging the mouse through the menu bar, releasing the left button selects the menu the pointer is on. Dragging the mouse along the menu bar while the pull-down menu is displayed has the same effect as using the $\rightarrow$ and $\leftarrow$ keys to move from one menu to another when the pull-down menu is displayed.

Note: If, while dragging the menu, you decide you do not want to select a menu, move the pointer to any area outside the menu bar or submenu box and release the left button. The menu is cleared. Also, at any point you can cancel the menu by clicking the right button.

Move the pointer to Help and click the left button. You have now selected the Help menu. This action has the same effect as typing the mnemonic letter of the menu.

Use the mouse to move the pointer to each of the three pull-down menu commands.

To select a pull-down menu command, move the pointer to the command (anywhere on the line within the menu box) and click the left button. You can also drag the mouse within the pull down-menu. This way you can see the submenu options associated with the highlighted pull-down menu command. When you release the left button the option is selected. Be careful when dragging the menus that you have the menu cursor on the correct menu item before releasing the left button.

Either method has the same effect as selecting the pull-down command using the arrow keys to highlight the command and pressing ⮐ , or by typing the mnemonic letter.

To select the Help command, move the pointer to Help and press the left button. Your screen should look similar to Figure 1-5, shown earlier

Note: If the pointer is not on a pull-down menu command when you select it, the menu bar is cleared from the screen. If this happens, click the right button again to re-display the menu bar and try again.

You have executed the Help menu's Help command. To exit the Help screen,

Click: Right button

This has the same effect as pressing ⮐ .

Using the Function Keys

The other way to issue a WordPerfect 5.1 command is to use the function keys. WordPerfect provides a function key template to place over the function keys to tell you what command each function key performs. If you have a function template place the appropriate template for your keyboard over the function keys.

Each function key, alone or in conjunction with other keys, can perform four different commands. The template lists the four commands associated with each function key. Notice that the commands are displayed in four colors. These colors tell you the key combinations to use to perform that specific task or activity. The color code and key combinations are explained below:

Color	Press
red	(CTRL) and function key
green	(SHIFT) and function key
blue	(ALT) and function key
black	function key alone

For example, (F3) used alone or in combination with (CTRL), (SHIFT), or (ALT), accesses four different WordPerfect commands, as shown below:

Key Combination	Command
(CTRL) - (F3)	Screen
(SHIFT) - (F3)	Switch
(ALT) - (F3)	Reveal Codes
(F3)	Help

The Help command, (F3), accesses the Help system as if you had selected Help from the menu bar and then Help from the pull-down menu of commands. To show how you can access Help using the Function key,

Press: Help (F3)

WORD PROCESSING

The same screen of information (Figure 1-5) about how to use the WordPerfect Help system is displayed. This time you will use Help to display information about the function key template on the screen (in case you do not have a template or lose or forget your template in the future). Following the directions on the Help screen to display the template,

Press: Help (F3)

Your display screen should be similar to Figure 1-6.

FIGURE 1-6

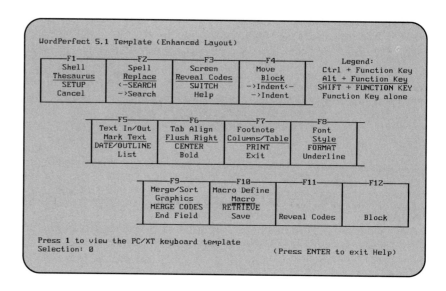

The Enhanced Layout template for keyboards whose function keys are above the typewriter keys is displayed.

If your function keys are located to the left of the typewriter section of the keyboard (PC/XT keyboard), following the directions on the screen,

Press: 1

The IBM PC/XT keyboard layout is displayed.

Depending upon your keyboard, the grid of 10 or 12 boxes displayed on the screen contains the WordPerfect commands that are associated with the function keys. Instead of a color code, the legend to the right lists the keys ((CTRL), (SHIFT) and (ALT)) that are used in combination with the function key, or the function key alone.

The function key template could also have been displayed using the pull-down menu by selecting Help and then Template.

To leave the Help screen,

Press: (⏎)

You are returned to the blank WordPerfect screen.

Note: If your template is a black and white photocopy of the template provided by WordPerfect, then use red, green, and blue highlight pens to color code your template.

Retrieving a File

Karen worked on the first draft of the welcome letter yesterday and saved it on the diskette in a file named LETTER.

To open a file in WordPerfect, the Retrieve command is used. To use the pull-down menu to select the Retrieve command,

Press: (ALT) - =

The Retrieve command is a command in the File menu. Because the menu cursor is already positioned over the File menu, to select it,

Press: (⏎)

The pull-down menu of 11 commands associated with the File menu is displayed. The Retrieve command is highlighted. To select the Retrieve command,

Press: (⏎)

Note: To cancel an incorrect menu selection, press (F1) (Cancel) to terminate the command, or (ESC) to back up one step in the command selection.

Your display screen should be similar to Figure 1-7.

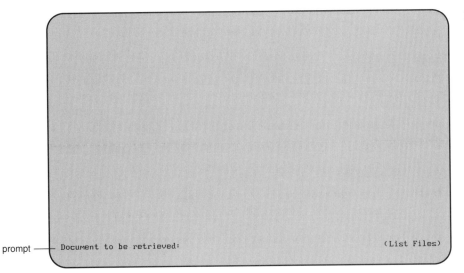

FIGURE 1-7

prompt —— Document to be retrieved: (List Files)

The cursor location information in the status line has been replaced by a WordPerfect prompt "Document to be retrieved." A **prompt** is the way the program tells you it needs more information. In this case the prompt wants you to enter the name of the file to be retrieved.

Before entering the file name, you will use Help for information about the Retrieve command. The WordPerfect Help system is **context-sensitive**. This means that whenever a command is in use, pressing Help ((F3)) will display information about that particular command.

Press: Help (F3)

Your display screen should be similar to Figure 1-8.

FIGURE 1-8

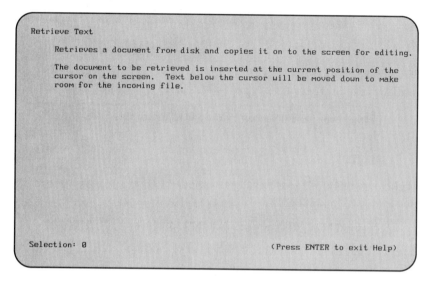

```
Retrieve Text

    Retrieves a document from disk and copies it on to the screen for editing.

    The document to be retrieved is inserted at the current position of the
    cursor on the screen.  Text below the cursor will be moved down to make
    room for the incoming file.




    Selection: 0                                      (Press ENTER to exit Help)
```

This screen tells you how the Retrieve command works. Most importantly it tells you that when you retrieve a file, a copy is displayed on the screen while the original file remains unchanged on the disk. The WordPerfect Help feature will provide specific information about the command you are using.

To leave the Help screen,

Press: ⏎

You are returned to the same place you were before using Help. You are now ready to enter the name of the file to retrieve. The file name can be entered in either upper- or lowercase letters. However, WordPerfect will always display a file name in uppercase.

Type: **LETTER**
Press: ⏎

After a few moments your display screen should be similar to Figure 1-9.

FIGURE 1-9

cursor

```
Deear Neew Spoorts Clubbb Meembeers:

Dongratullatiooons on on on your new membership membership in the
Spoorts Club.  Allll of us on the the staff welcome welcome you
and encourage you you to participate innnn the many
tournamentssss, leagues and club activitieeees offffered
throughjout the yearr.

Each monthhh you wil will redeive a newsletter avout the upcoming
eventsss at the culg.  If you have  about the event or would lime
to sighn up up up to particiapte in an efent, just or come ininin
to the fromt desk personnelll.

The club facilities include 18 lighted tennis courst × ×× ××××××
5 racquetball courts, an olympic size swimming 77777 www gggggggg
pool, Nautilus equipped weight room, and basketball court.  For
JJJJJJJ BBBB $$$$$$$ cYYYYY tttttt(( )))))) $$$$$$ @@@@@@@
rrrrrrrr  IIIII uUUUUU ××××××× bbbbb GGGGGGG DDDDDD 444444
444444 jjjjjjjbb   ccccc ddtydrdh yryygh hgdd rrssrt nkhu 87t56rf
tfhghgr 6f fhgf 5dggf645hgh  hghtyuj ygyt fdfd uuuuyty ghddfh
your comfort while using the club, the men's and ladies' locker
rooms

  each have showers, a sauna, and a steam steam room.  A spa for
B:\LETTER                                    Doc 1 Pg 1 Ln 1" Pos 1"
```

file name

The Retrieve command loads a copy of the file from the diskette into memory. The original file remains on the diskette. The first three paragraphs of the rough draft of the welcome letter are displayed on the screen. As you can see, it contains many errors, which you will correct in this lab.

In addition to the cursor location information, the status line displays the file name of the file in use. This information will sometimes be replaced with other WordPerfect messages. Often a prompt (like the one you responded to when retrieving the file) or a menu of choices to select from will be displayed in the status line as part of the command sequence. Again, if you find that you have entered an incorrect command and are accidentally in the wrong menu, press Cancel ((F1)) or (ESC). Then reenter the command correctly.

You could have also entered this command using the function key combination, (SHIFT) - (F10). Look on your template next to the (F10) key. The word "Retrieve" is printed in green letters. The top left-hand corner of the template displays the color code. Green means to use (SHIFT) in combination with the function key (hold down (SHIFT) and, while holding it down, press (F10)).

Moving the Cursor

The cursor can be moved around the screen by using the arrow keys or by using the mouse. The arrow keys, located on the numeric keypad or on the separate cursor key area, move the cursor one character space in the direction indicated by the arrow.

Note: Be careful to use only the keys specified as you are following the directions in this section. If you do, the instructions and figures in the text should be the same as what you see on your screen. Also, make sure the (NUM LOCK) (number lock) key is not on when using the numeric keypad area. If it is, numbers will be entered on the screen rather than the cursor moving through the text.

Press: (→) (6 times)

Your display screen should be similar to Figure 1-10.

FIGURE 1-10

```
Deear Neew Spoorts Clubbb Meembeers:

Dongratullatiooons on on on your new membership membership in the
Spoorts Club.  Allll of us on the the staff welcome welcome you
and encourage you you to participate innnn the many
tournamentssss, leagues and club activitieeees offffered
throughjout the yearr.

Each monthhh you wil will redeive a newsletter avout the upcoming
eventsss at the culg.  If you have  about the event or would lime
to sighn up up up to particiapte in an efent, just or come ininin
to the fromt desk personnelll.

The club facilities include 18 lighted tennis courst × ×× ××××××
5 racquetball courts, an olympic size swimming 77777 www gggggggg
pool, Nautilus equipped weight room, and basketball court.  For
JJJJJJJ BBBB $$$$$$ cYYYYY tttttt(( )))))  $$$$$$  @@@@@@
rrrrrrrr  IIIII uUUUUU ××××××× bbbbb GGGGGGG DDDDDD 444444
444444 jjjjjjjbb   ccccc ddtydrdh yryygh hgdd rrssrt nkhu 87t56rf
tfhghgr 6f fhgf 5dggf645hgh  hghtyuj ygyt fdfd uuuuyty ghddfh
your comfort while using the club, the men's and ladies' locker
rooms

 each have showers, a sauna, and a steam steam room.  A spa for
B:\LETTER                              Doc 1 Pg 1 Ln 1" Pos 1.6"
```

cursor

new
position
value

The cursor moved six character spaces to the right along the line. It should be positioned under the "N" in "Neew." Notice how the status line reflects the change in the horizontal location of the cursor on the line. The position value increased to 1.6" as the cursor moved to the right along the line. The position value is displayed as a decimal. The current cursor location then is 1-6/10 inch from the left edge of the page.

Press:

The cursor moved down one line. Since this is a blank line, the cursor moved back to the left margin on the line. The status line reflects the change in the location of the cursor by telling you that the new vertical or line location of the cursor is Ln 1.17", and the horizontal location of the cursor is Pos 1". Like the position value, the line value is displayed as a decimal. Line numbers increase as you move down the page. The current line location of the cursor is 1-17/100 inch from the top of the page.

Press:

The cursor moved down to the next line and back to Pos 1.6". It should be on the "t" in "Dongratullatiooons." The cursor moved to position 1.6 because it was last located in a line containing text (line 1") at that position. The cursor will attempt to maintain its position in a line of text as you move up or down through the document.

By holding down either ← or →, the cursor will move quickly character by character along the line.

To see how this works, hold down → and move the cursor to the right along the line until it is under the "i" in the word "in."

The status line should show that the cursor is on Pos 6.9". If you moved too far to the right along the line of text, use ← to move back to the correct position.

This saves multiple presses of the arrow key. Many of the WordPerfect cursor movement keys can be held down to execute multiple moves.

Press: ↑ (2 times)

The cursor moved up two lines and should be positioned at the end of the first line.
Using the arrow keys and the status line for cursor location reference,

Move to: Ln 3.17" Pos 7.4" (end of first line of third paragraph)

Note: Throughout the WordPerfect 5.1 labs you will be instructed to move the cursor to specific line and position locations (for example, Move to: Ln 3.17" Pos 7.4"). To confirm the appropriate cursor position, the location of the cursor in the text is described in parentheses (for example, "end of first line of third paragraph"). If your cursor is not at the described location, move it there before continuing.

The default right margin setting is 1 inch from the right side of the paper (Pos 7.5".) To see what happens when the cursor reaches the right margin,

Press: $\rightarrow$

The cursor automatically moved to the beginning of the next line. Unlike a typewriter, you did not need to press a return key to move from the end of one line to the beginning of the next. It is done automatically for you.
You can also move the cursor word by word in either direction on a line by using (CTRL) in combination with $\rightarrow$ or $\leftarrow$. (CTRL) is held down while pressing the arrow key.

Press: (CTRL) - $\rightarrow$ (5 times)

The cursor skipped to the beginning of each word and moved five words to the right along the line. It should be positioned on the "s" in the word "size."
To move back to the first word in this line,

Press: (CTRL) - $\leftarrow$ (5 times)

The cursor should be positioned on "5," the first character in the line. If the cursor is positioned in the middle of a word, (CTRL) - $\rightarrow$ will move the cursor to the beginning of the next word; however, (CTRL) - $\leftarrow$ will move the cursor to the beginning of the word it is on, rather than to the beginning of the preceding word.
The cursor can be moved quickly to the end of a line of text by pressing (END). To move to the end of this line,

Press: (END)

Pressing (HOME) and then $\rightarrow$ will have the same effect. But it requires the use of two keys rather than one.
Unfortunately, simply pressing (HOME) will not take you to the beginning of a line of text. Because (HOME) is used in combination with several other keys, you must use it followed by $\leftarrow$ to move to the beginning of a line.
To move back to the beginning of the line,

Press: (HOME)
Press: $\leftarrow$

The cursor should be back on the "5."

The letter is longer than what is currently displayed on the screen. To move to the bottom line of the screen, using ⬇,

Move to: Ln 4.83" Pos 1" (beginning of the first line of the fourth paragraph)

The screen can display only 24 lines of text at a time. If the cursor is positioned on either the top or bottom line of the screen, using ⬆ or ⬇ will move, or **scroll**, more lines of the document onto the screen. As you scroll up or down through the document, the lines at the top or bottom of the screen move out of view to allow more text to be displayed.

To scroll the rest of the letter into view on the screen,

Press: ⬇ (13 times)

The cursor should be at the beginning of the word "Sports" (Ln 7").

Your display screen should be similar to Figure 1-11.

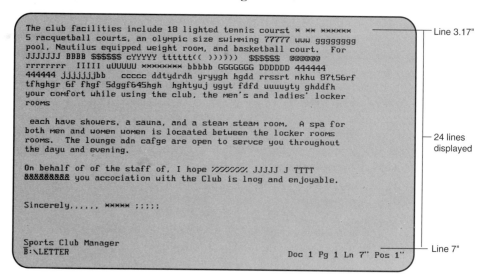

```
The club facilities include 18 lighted tennis courst × ×× ××××××      Line 3.17"
5 racquetball courts, an olympic size swimming 77777 uuu ggggggggg
pool, Nautilus equipped weight room, and basketball court.  For
JJJJJJJ BBBB $$$$$$ cYYYYY tttttt(( )))))  $$$$$$  @@@@@@
rrrrrrrr  IIIII uUUUUU ×××××××× bbbbb GGGGGGG DDDDDD 444444
444444 jjjjjjjbb   ccccc ddtydrdh yryygh hgdd rrssrt nkhu 87t56rf
tfhghgr 6f fhgf 5dggf645hgh  hghtyuj ygyt fdfd uuuuyty ghddfh
your comfort while using the club, the men's and ladies' locker
rooms

 each have showers, a sauna, and a steam steam room.  A spa for
both men and women women is locaated between the locker rooms     24 lines
rooms.  The lounge adn cafge are open to servce you throughout     displayed
the dayu and evening.

On behalf of of the staff of, I hope ////////. JJJJJ J TTTT
&&&&&&&&& you accociation with the Club is lnog and enjoyable.

Sincerely,...... ××××× ;;;;;



Sports Club Manager
B:\LETTER                                                         Line 7"
                                 Doc 1 Pg 1 Ln 7" Pos 1"
```

FIGURE 1-11

The first 13 lines of the letter are no longer visible on the screen. They scrolled off the top of the screen to allow the new lines at the bottom of the screen to be displayed.

Each time you pressed ⬇ a new line of text was brought into view at the bottom of the screen. At the same time a line of text scrolled out of view at the top of the screen.

The screen still displays only 24 lines of the letter. The cursor can be moved quickly to the top line of the screen by pressing (HOME) followed by ⬆. To move to the top line of the screen,

Press: (HOME)
Press: ⬆

The cursor should be at the beginning of Ln 3.17", on the "t" in "the."

(HOME) followed by ↓ will move the cursor to the last line of the screen.

WP23
Moving the Cursor

Press: (HOME)
Press: ↓

The cursor should be positioned back at the beginning of "Sports" on the last line (Ln 7") of the screen.

You can also move to the top or bottom of the screen by using the minus (-) or plus (+) signs located to the right of the numeric keypad. (Do not use the plus or minus signs located in the upper row of the keyboard.) To move to the top of the screen,

Press: -

The cursor is positioned back on the first line of text on the screen.

Press: +

The cursor is positioned back on the last line of the screen.

Using the plus or minus keys to move to the bottom or top of the screen requires fewer keystrokes than using (HOME) and ↑ or ↓.

The screen is positioned over 24 lines of text on page 1 of the document (see Figure 1-11). WordPerfect differentiates between a screen and a page. A screen can display only 24 lines of text, whereas the printed page can display many more lines of text.

The cursor can be moved to the top or bottom line of a page using the (CTRL)-(HOME) key combination (while holding down (CTRL) press (HOME)). This is called the Go to key because of the prompt you will see displayed in status line.

Press: (CTRL)-(HOME)

Your display screen should be similar to Figure 1-12.

FIGURE 1-12

```
The club facilities include 18 lighted tennis courst × ×× ××××××
5 racquetball courts, an olympic size swimming 77777 www gggggggg
pool, Nautilus equipped weight room, and basketball court.  For
JJJJJJJ BBBB $$$$$$ cYYYYY tttttt(( )))))  $$$$$$  @@@@@@
rrrrrrrr  IIIII uUUUUU ×××××××× bbbbb GGGGGGG DDDDDD 444444
444444 jjjjjjjbb   ccccc ddtydrdh yryygh hgdd rrssrt nkhu 87t56rf
tfhghgr 6f fhgf 5dggf645hgh  hghtyuj ygyt fdfd uuuuyty ghddfh
your comfort while using the club, the men's and ladies' locker
rooms

 each have showers, a sauna, and a steam steam room.  A spa for
both men and women women is loacated between the locker rooms
rooms.  The lounge adn cafge are open to servce you throughout
the dayu and evening.

On behalf of of the staff of, I hope ///////. JJJJJ J TTTT
&&&&&&&&& you accociation with the Club is lnog and enjoyable.

Sincerely,,,,,, ××××× ;;;;;

Sports Club Manager
Go to _
```

prompt

The prompt "Go to" is displayed in the status line. A number, a character, ⊙ or ⊙ can be entered at this prompt.

To move to the top of the current page,

Press: ⊙

The cursor should be positioned on the first line (1") of page 1. The screen is positioned over the first 24 lines of text on this page.

To move the cursor to the last line of page 1,

Press: (CTRL) - (HOME)
Press: ⊙

The cursor should be positioned on the last line of page 1. The dashed line at the bottom of the screen shows the location of the end of page 1 and the beginning of page 2.

Press: ⊙

Your display screen should be similar to Figure 1-13.

FIGURE 1-13

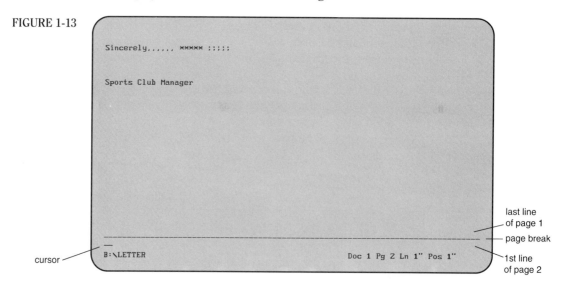

The cursor should be positioned on the last line of the screen. This is the first line of page 2 in the document.

The cursor can also be quickly moved from one page of text to another using the (PGUP) (page up) and (PGDN) (page down) keys. The message "Repositioning" will appear briefly in the status line while the cursor moves to the new location.

To move back to the top of the previous page,

Press: (PGUP)

The cursor is positioned on the first line of page 1.

To move to the top of page 2,

Press: (PGDN)

Your display screen should be similar to Figure 1-14.

FIGURE 1-14

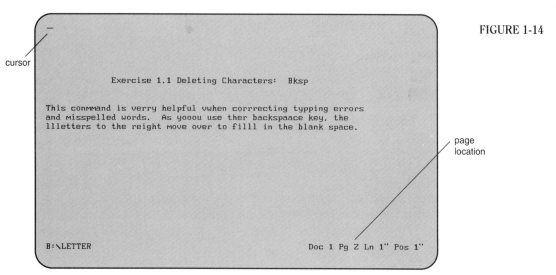

The cursor should be on the first line of page 2. The screen is positioned over the first 24 lines of page 2. Using (PGUP) or (PGDN) always positions the cursor on the left margin of the first line of the page.

To move through several pages of the document at once, you could press (PGDN) or (PGUP) multiple times. Or you can use the GoTo key combination again.

To move to page 5 of this document,

Press: (CTRL) - (HOME)

To respond to the "Go to" prompt, enter the page number. Use the number keys on the top line of the keyboard, above the alphabetic keys, as follows:

Type: 5
Press: (⏎)

Your display screen should be similar to Figure 1-15.

FIGURE 1-15

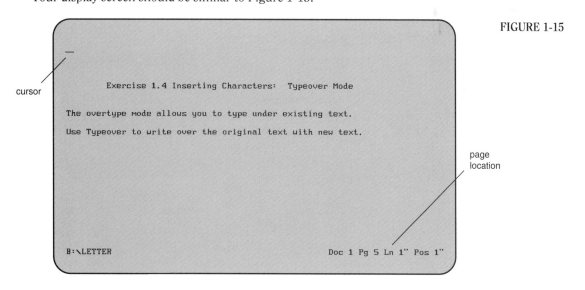

WORD PROCESSING

The cursor is positioned on the first line of page 5.

The biggest jump the cursor can make is to move to the beginning or end of a document. To move to the end of this document,

Press: (HOME)
Press: (HOME)
Press: (↓)

Your display screen should be similar to Figure 1-16.

FIGURE 1-16

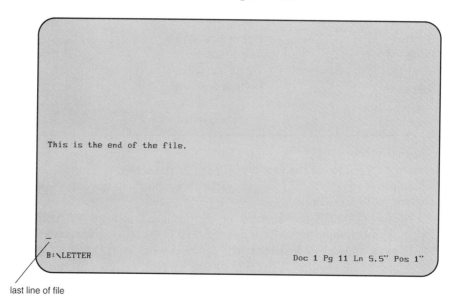

```
                This is the end of the file.




B:\LETTER                                    Doc 1 Pg 11 Ln 5.5" Pos 1"
```

last line of file

The cursor should be positioned on a blank line. This line is the last line in the document.

To move quickly back to the first line of text in the document,

Press: (HOME)
Press: (HOME)
Press: (↑)

The cursor should be positioned on the first line of page 1 of this document.

To review, the following cursor movement features have been covered:

Key	Action
→	One character to right
←	One character to left
↑	One line up
↓	One line down
CTRL - →	One word to right
CTRL - ←	One word to left
HOME - →	Right end of line
END	Right end of line
HOME, ←	Left edge of screen
HOME, ↑	Top of screen
- (minus sign)	Top of screen
HOME, ↓	Bottom of screen
[+] (plus sign)	Bottom of screen
CTRL - HOME, ↑	Top of current page
CTRL - HOME, ↓	Bottom of current page
CTRL - HOME page number	Top of page number specified
PGUP	Top of previous page
PGDN	Top of next page
HOME, HOME, ↑	Beginning of document
HOME, HOME, ↓	End of document

Using the Mouse to Move the Cursor

If you do not have a mouse, skip to the next section, "Editing a Document." If you have a mouse, you can use it to move the cursor to a specific location in a document. To do this, position the mouse pointer at the location in the text where you want to move the cursor and click the left button. Using the mouse,

Move to: "y" of "your" (first line of first paragraph)

Notice the cursor has not moved and the status line information has not changed.

Click: left button

The cursor is now positioned under the "y," and the status line reflects its new location in the document (Ln 1.33" Pos 3.8").

Practice using the mouse to move the cursor by moving it to the following locations on the screen:

Move to: "E" in "Each" (first line of second paragraph)

Move to: "b" in "basketball" (third line of third paragraph)

Move to: "s" in "sauna" (last line on screen)

Try moving the mouse pointer to the next line of text.

It will not move beyond the displayed text on the screen. To scroll the text on the screen, with the mouse pointer positioned on either the top or bottom line of the text on the screen, hold down the right button and move the mouse slightly up or down. The screen will continue to scroll until you release the button.

To try this, with the mouse positioned on the last line of text on the screen (not the status line) hold down the right button and move the mouse downward. Be careful that you do not quickly click the right button, as this will cause the menu to be displayed. If this happens, click the right button again to cancel the menu.

After a moment to stop the scrolling, release the right button.

Upon releasing the right button, the cursor also moves to the mouse pointer location. If there is no text on the line where you stopped scrolling, the cursor will be positioned at the beginning of the line.

Scroll the document upward until you are back on the first line of text on page 1.

To review, the following mouse features have been covered:

Mouse	Action
In Editing screen:	
Click right button	Displays menu.
Click left button	Positions cursor.
Dragging - right button	Scrolls screen.
In pull-down menus:	
Click right button	Backs out of all menus and removes menu bar from screen.
Click left button	Displays menu choices for menu-bar item positioned on or selects menu item.
Dragging	Moves across menu-bar and displays pull-down menu for each of the nine menus.
	Moves down a pull-down menu,highlights each choice and displays submenu if available. Releasing the button selects the highlighted command.

Editing a Document

Now that you have learned how to move the cursor around the document, you are ready to learn how to **edit**, or correct errors in a document.

The next part of this lab contains a series of exercises. Each exercise will show you a WordPerfect editing feature and allow you to practice using the feature. As you read the text in the book you will be directed to use the editing feature to correct the exercise on your display screen. When you have completed the exercise, a figure in the book will show you how your display screen should appear. After completing each exercise press (PGDN) to go to the next exercise. To begin the exercise,

Press: (PGDN)

Exercise 1.1 Deleting Characters: (BKSP)

Your display screen should be similar to Figure 1-17.

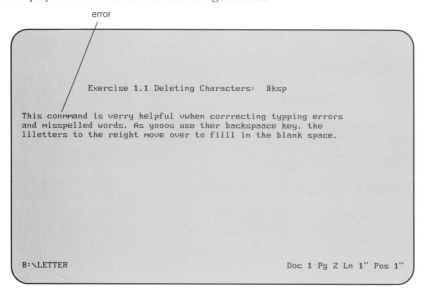

FIGURE 1-17

The first exercise, "Exercise 1.1 Deleting Characters: Bksp," should be on your display screen.

The (BKSP) (backspace) key will **delete,** or erase, a character to the left of the cursor. This key may be labeled with a left-facing arrow, the word "Backspace" or "Bksp," or a combination of the two. It is located above the ⟵ key.

The paragraph in the exercise on the display screen contains several errors that you will correct using the (BKSP) key. The first error on the screen is in the second word, "conmmand." The word should be "command." The "n" needs to be deleted.

To position the cursor to the right of the "n,"

Move to: Ln 2.33" Pos 1.8" (first "m" in "conmmand")

Note: If you are using the mouse to move the cursor, use the information in parentheses to tell you where to position the mouse pointer. Then verify the cursor position using the line and position information.

As a character is deleted, the text to the right will move over to fill in the space left by the deleted character. Watch your screen carefully as you

Press: (BKSP)

The character to the left of the cursor, in this case the "n", is deleted. The text to the right then moves over one space to fill in the space left by the character that was deleted.

There is now an extra space at the end of this line. As soon as you move the cursor to the right one space or down a line, WordPerfect will examine the line to see whether the word beginning on the next line ("and") can be moved up to fill in the space without exceeding the margin setting. This process of filling in the spaces is called **reformatting**. Watch your screen carefully as you correct the error in the word "verry."

Move to:	Ln 2.33" Pos 2.9" (second "r" in "verry")
Press:	(BKSP)
Press:	(→) (1 time)

Your display screen should look similar to Figure 1-18.

FIGURE 1-18

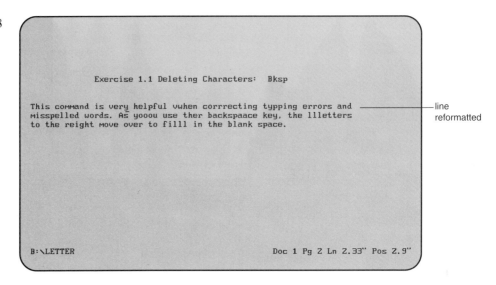

```
                 Exercise 1.1 Deleting Characters:  Bksp


This command is very helpful vvhen corrrecting typping errors and ──────── line
misspelled words. As yooou use ther backspaace key, the llletters            reformatted
to the reight move over to filll in the blank space.




B:\LETTER                                        Doc 1 Pg 2 Ln 2.33" Pos 2.9"
```

The word "and" from the beginning of the line below moved up to the end of the current line. The deletion of the extra characters created enough space for the whole word to move up a line. As you move the cursor through the text it will be automatically reformatted.

The automatic reformatting of text is the default setting in WordPerfect 5.1. As you move through the text the lines above the cursor will always display properly on the screen.

Continue this exercise by using (BKSP) to correct the text on the display. As you edit and move through the text, WordPerfect will constantly reexamine the margin space and reformat as needed.

When you are finished your display screen should be similar to Figure 1-19.

FIGURE 1-19

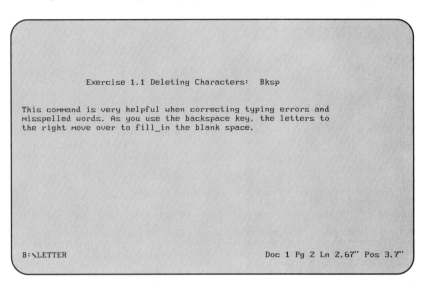

```
          Exercise 1.1 Deleting Characters:  Bksp

This command is very helpful when correcting typing errors and
misspelled words. As you use the backspace key, the letters to
the right move over to fill_in the blank space.




B:\LETTER                          Doc 1 Pg 2 Ln 2.67" Pos 3.7"
```

As you can see, each time you press (BKSP) the cursor "backs up" through the text, deleting the character to the left of the cursor. The text is reformatted as needed.

Exercise 1.2 Deleting Characters: (DEL)

To move to the next exercise,

Press: (PGDN)

The second exercise, "Exercise 1.2 Deleting Characters: Del," should be on your screen.

A second way to delete a character is with (DEL). On most keyboards the (DEL) key is at the right side of the keyboard beneath the numeric keypad. This key will delete the character the cursor is positioned under.

The first error is in the second word in the first line of the exercise, "**u**you."

Move to: Ln 2.67" Pos 1.5" (under the first "u" in "uyou")

To delete the "u,"

Press: (DEL)

The "u" was removed, and the text to the right moved over to fill in the blank space. The paragraph will be reformatted as needed.

Complete the exercise by using (DEL) to correct the text on the screen. When you are done your display screen should be similar to Figure 1-20 on the next page.

WORD PROCESSING

```
          Exercise 1.2 Deleting Characters:   Del

When you use the Del key, the character under the cursor is
deleted. This command is useful when you see an error in the text
several lines back. Instead of using the backspace key and
deleting all the correct text, use the arrow keys to move the
cursor to the location of the error, and press Del.

As the characters are deleted, the text from the right fills in
the blank space.




B:\LETTER                              Doc 1 Pg 3 Ln 3.33" Pos 4.3"
```

FIGURE 1-20

Exercise 1.3 Inserting Characters: Insert Mode

Press: (PGDN)

Text can be entered into a document in either the **Insert** or **Typeover modes**. The default setting for WordPerfect is the Insert mode. As you type in Insert mode, new characters are inserted into the existing text. The existing text moves to the right to make space for the new characters.

The first sentence on the screen should read: "The **Insert** mode allows new text **to** be entered into **a** document." The three missing words, "Insert," "to" and "a" can be easily entered into the sentence without retyping it.

To enter the word "Insert" before the word "mode" in the first sentence,

Move to:	Ln 3" Pos 1.4" (under the "m" in "mode")
Type:	**Insert**
Press:	Space bar

The word "Insert" has been entered into the sentence by moving everything to the right to make space as each letter is typed.

Next, to enter the word "to" before the word "be,"

Move to:	Line 3" Pos 4.2" (under the "b" in "be")
Type:	**to**
Press:	Space bar

Finally, to enter the word "a" before the word "document,"

Move to:	Ln 3" Pos 6.1" (under the "d" in "document")
Type:	**a**
Press:	Space bar

Your display screen should be similar to Figure 1-21.

FIGURE 1-21

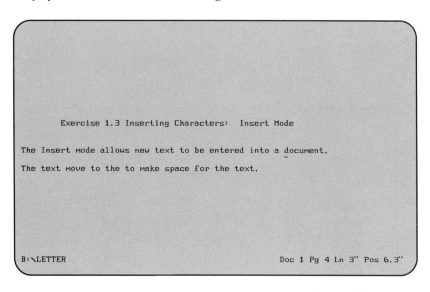

```
        Exercise 1.3 Inserting Characters:  Insert Mode

The Insert mode allows new text to be entered into a document.

The text move to the to make space for the text.
```

B:\LETTER   Doc 1 Pg 4 Ln 3" Pos 6.3"

As each new character was entered into the existing text, the text to the right moved over to make space.

In a similar manner, correct the second sentence on the screen to read: "The **old** text move**s** to the **right** to make space for the **new** text". Your display screen should be similar to Figure 1-22.

FIGURE 1-22

```
        Exercise 1.3 Inserting Characters:  Insert Mode

The Insert mode allows new text to be entered into a document.

The old text moves to the right to make space for the new text.
```

B:\LETTER   Doc 1 Pg 4 Ln 3.33" Pos 6.8"

Exercise 1.4 Inserting Characters: Typeover Mode

Press: (PGDN)

The second method of entering text in a document is to use the Typeover mode. In this mode, the new text types over the existing characters.

WORD PROCESSING

The (INS) (insert) key, located to the left of the (DEL) key, changes the mode from Insert to Typeover.

Press: (INS)

Your display screen should be similar to Figure 1-23.

FIGURE 1-23

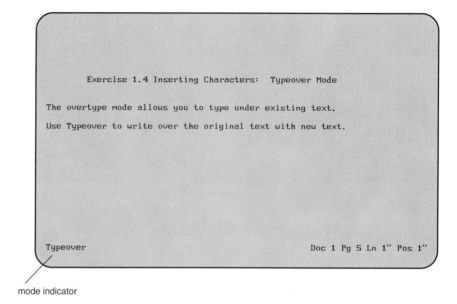

```
                    Exercise 1.4 Inserting Characters:  Typeover Mode

     The overtype mode allows you to type under existing text.
     Use Typeover to write over the original text with new text.




     Typeover                                        Doc 1 Pg 5 Ln 1" Pos 1"
```

mode indicator

To tell you that the Typeover mode is on, the word "Typeover" appears on the left side of the status line.

The first sentence should read: "The **Typeover** mode allows you to type **over** existing text." To correct this sentence,

Move to: Ln 2.5" Pos 1.4" (beginning of "overtype")
Type: **Typeover**

As each character was typed, the character (or space) under it was replaced with the character being typed.

Next, to replace the word "under" with "over,"

Move to: Ln 2.5" Pos 4.7" (beginning of "under")
Type: **over**

Notice that there is still one extra character. To remove the extra "r,"

Press: (DEL)

Your display screen should be similar to Figure 1-24.

FIGURE 1-24

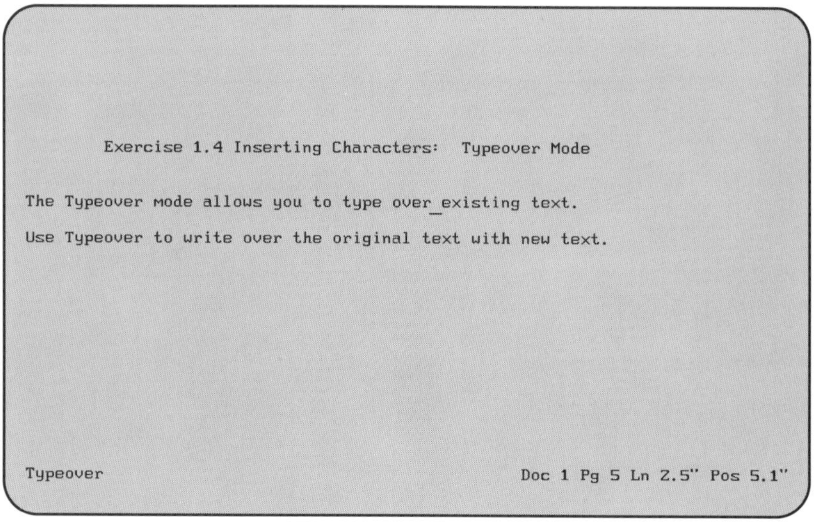

```
      Exercise 1.4 Inserting Characters:   Typeover Mode

The Typeover mode allows you to type over_existing text.

Use Typeover to write over the original text with new text.




Typeover                                    Doc 1 Pg 5 Ln 2.5" Pos 5.1"
```

In a similar manner, correct the sentence to be: "**The** typeover **mode replaces the** original text with new text."

To turn off the Typeover mode,

Press: (INS)

Exercise 1.5 Deleting Words: (CTRL) - (BKSP)

Press: (PGDN)

The (CTRL) - (BKSP) key combination is used to delete entire words. The cursor can be positioned on any character of the word to be deleted, or one space to the left of the word to be deleted.

The first line on the screen contains several duplicate words. It should read: "This command is very helpful for deleting unnecessary words."

To remove the first duplicate word, "command,"

Move to: Ln 2.67" Pos 1.5" ("c" of "command")
Press: (CTRL) - (BKSP)

The word the cursor is positioned on is deleted. Notice also that one blank space was deleted, leaving the correct number of spaces between words.

If the cursor is placed on a blank space immediately after a word, then using (CTRL) - (BKSP) deletes the word to the left of the cursor and the blank space the cursor is on.

Use (CTRL) - (BKSP) to delete the other duplicate words in the sentences on the screen. After completing the exercise, your display screen should be similar to Figure 1-25.

FIGURE 1-25

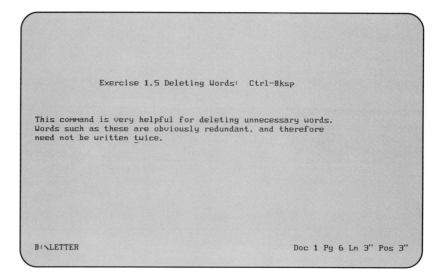

```
                        Exercise 1.5 Deleting Words:   Ctrl-Bksp


        This command is very helpful for deleting unnecessary words.
        Words such as these are obviously redundant, and therefore
        need not be written twice.
                               _




    B:\LETTER                                      Doc 1 Pg 6 Ln 3" Pos 3"
```

The text to the right filled in the blank space when you deleted a word. The paragraph was reformatted as needed. You may have also noticed that any punctuation following a word is considered part of the word and is deleted also.

Exercise 1.6 Deleting from Cursor to End of Line: (CTRL) - (END)

Press: (PGDN)

The (CTRL) - (END) key combination will delete everything on a line from the cursor to the right. If the cursor is placed at the beginning of a line, all the text on the line is deleted.

You will delete the unnecessary text following the word "cursor" in the first line in this exercise.

Move to: Ln 2.67" Pos 4.5" (first "8" immediately following "cursor")
Press: (CTRL) - (END)

The text from the cursor to the right is deleted.

Continue this exercise by deleting the unnecessary characters at the end of the next two lines.

Next, delete the entire contents of the fourth line by placing the cursor on the first character in the line.

Your display screen should be similar to Figure 1-26.

```
┌─────────────────────────────────────────────────────────┐
│                                                           │
│                                                           │
│                                                           │
│   Exercise 1.6  Deleting From Cursor to End of Line:  Ctrl-End  │
│                                                           │
│   To delete the text from the cursor                      │
│   to the end of the line,                                 │
│   move the cursor to the first character                  │
│   ▃                                                       │
│   you want to delete and press Ctrl-End.                  │
│                                                           │
│                                                           │
│                                                           │
│                                                           │
│                                                           │
│                                                           │
│   B:\LETTER               Doc 1 Pg 7 Ln 3.17" Pos 1"      │
└─────────────────────────────────────────────────────────┘
```

FIGURE 1-26

Exercise 1.7 Deleting Several Lines of Text: (ESC), (CTRL) - (END)

Press: (PGDN)

Several lines of text can be deleted at once by using (ESC) followed by the (CTRL) - (END) key combination. To delete several lines of text, first move the cursor to the beginning of the line of text to be deleted.

To erase the lines which are labeled as lines 13, 14, and 15 on the screen, first,

Move to: Ln 3" Pos 1" (beginning of line 13)

Next, count the number of lines you want to erase. You want to delete three lines. To do this, you could use the (CTRL) - (END) command three times to erase the contents of each line. Or you can use (ESC) to tell WordPerfect to repeat a function a specified number of times.

Press: (ESC)

The status line displays the prompt "Repeat Value = 8." The number 8 is the default setting.

(ESC) acts as a **repeater** to specify the number of times to repeat a specified function. The number you enter tells WordPerfect how many times to repeat the function you will enter next. Do not press (⏎) after typing in your response to the prompt.

To repeat the function three times,

Type: 3

There are many functions which can be repeated. To move through a document you can press (ESC) and the (↑) and (↓) keys to move up or down a specified number of lines, (PGUP) or (PGDN) to move forward or backward by pages, (→) or (←) to move right or left character by character along a line. To delete text you can press (ESC) and (CTRL) - (BKSP) to remove a specified number of words, (CTRL) - (END) to remove lines of text, or (CTRL) - (PGDN) to delete pages. In this case, to remove the three lines of text,

Press: (CTRL) - (END)

Your display screen should be similar to Figure 1-27.

FIGURE 1-27

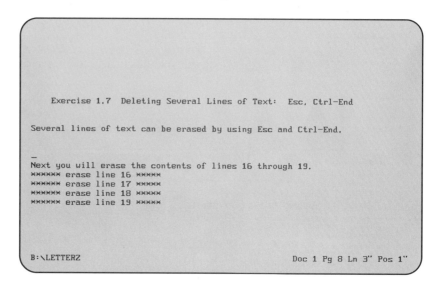

The contents of lines 13, 14, and 15 have been deleted.
 In a similar manner, erase lines 16 through 19.
 (ESC) can be entered before using the arrow and (DEL) keys, (PGUP) , (PGDN) , (HOME)- (↓) and (HOME) - (↑), and (CTRL) - (←) and (CTRL) - (→) to tell WordPerfect to repeat the procedure the specified number of times. It can also be used to enter the same character into the text a number of times.

Exercise 1.8 Inserting and Deleting Blank Lines

Press: (PGDN)

The (←┘) key is used to insert a blank line into text or to mark the end of a paragraph. It is called a **hard carriage return**
 If (←┘) is pressed in the middle of a line of text, all text to the right of the cursor moves to the beginning of the next line. For example,

Move to: Ln 2.5" Pos 5.3 ("m" of "middle" in the first line of this exercise)
Press: (←┘)

A hard carriage return is entered at the end of the first line, and the text from the cursor to the right moves down to the beginning of the next line.

If you press (BKSP) the hard carriage return at the end of the first line is deleted, and the text returns to its original location.

Press: (BKSP)

If ⏎ is pressed at the beginning of a line, a blank line is inserted into the document. To see how this works,

Move to: Ln 3" Pos 1" (beginning of "If" on the fourth line of this exercise)
Press: ⏎

A blank line is inserted into the text, forcing the line the cursor is on to move down one line.

If ⏎ is pressed at the end of a paragraph or line of text, the cursor moves to the beginning of the next line.

Move to: Ln 3.83" Pos 7.5" (end of last line in the exercise)
Press: ⏎

The cursor moves to the beginning of the next line.

To delete a blank line, position the cursor at the beginning of the blank line and press (DEL). To try this,

Move to: Ln 3.5" Pos 1" (beginning of blank line between second and third sentences)
Press: (DEL)

Your display screen should be similar to Figure 1-28.

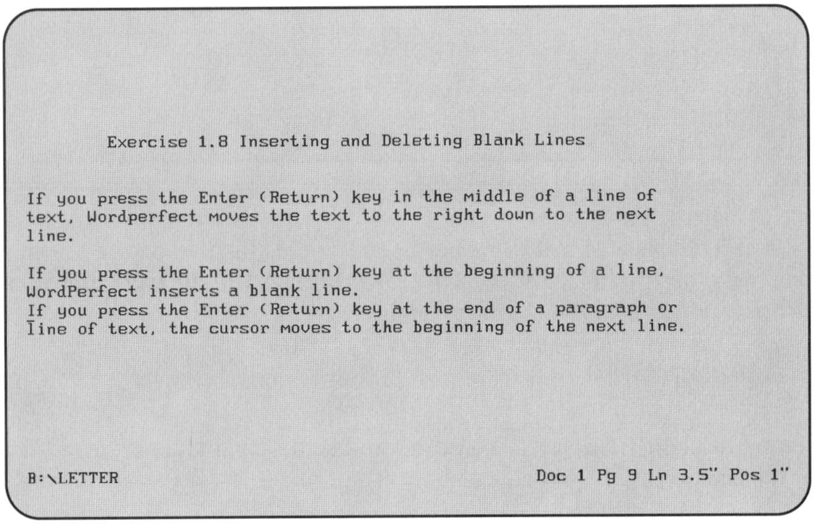

FIGURE 1-28

```
         Exercise 1.8 Inserting and Deleting Blank Lines

  If you press the Enter (Return) key in the middle of a line of
  text, Wordperfect moves the text to the right down to the next
  line.

  If you press the Enter (Return) key at the beginning of a line,
  WordPerfect inserts a blank line.
  If you press the Enter (Return) key at the end of a paragraph or
  line of text, the cursor moves to the beginning of the next line.




  B:\LETTER                           Doc 1 Pg 9 Ln 3.5" Pos 1"
```

The blank line is deleted, and the text below moves up one line.

Exercise 1.9 Undeleting Text

Press: (PGDN)

It is easy to accidentally delete text you did not intend to delete. Fortunately the Edit>Undelete, or Undelete (F1), command lets you restore your deletions. To do this, each time you delete text WordPerfect stores it in a special file called a **buffer**. Only the last three deletions are stored.

To see how this works, delete the three sentences numbered 1, 2, and 3 by moving to the beginning of each line and pressing (CTRL) - (END).

To restore the deleted text,

Select: Edit
Select: Undelete

Your screen should be similar to Figure 1-29.

FIGURE 1-29

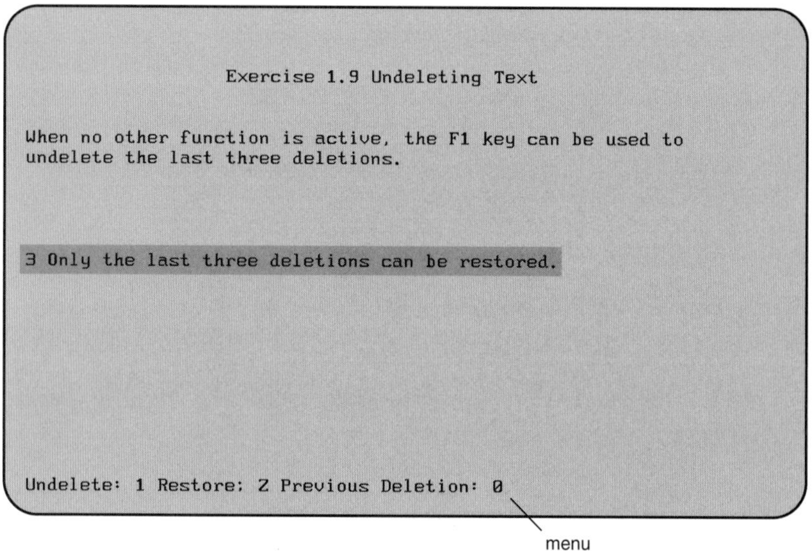

```
                    Exercise 1.9 Undeleting Text


    When no other function is active, the F1 key can be used to
    undelete the last three deletions.



   3 Only the last three deletions can be restored.









   Undelete: 1 Restore: 2 Previous Deletion: 0
```

menu

The most recently deleted text (sentence 3) appears highlighted on the screen. The undelete menu appears in the status line. It lets you restore the highlighted text or see the previous deletions. To see the previous deletion,

Select: Previous

The second deletion is displayed. You can also use the up and down arrow keys to display the deletions.

Press: (↑)

The first deletion is displayed.

Press: (↑)

The third deletion is displayed again. To restore the highlighted text,

Select: Restore

The third deletion is reentered at the cursor position.

Restore the first and second deletions in numerical order above sentence 3. To do this, first position the cursor in the location where you want the text displayed. Then select the Edit>Undelete command, display the deleted text, and select Restore. When you are done the screen should appear as it did before you deleted the sentences.

To review, the following editing keys have been covered:

Key	Action
(BKSP)	Deletes character to left of cursor
(DEL)	Deletes character at cursor
(INS) on	Inserts character into text
(INS) off	Uses Typeover mode to insert text
(CTRL) - (BKSP)	Deletes word cursor is on
(↵)	Moves cursor to next line
	Inserts a blank line
(CTRL) - (END)	Deletes line of text from cursor to right
(ESC) # (function)	Repeats certain functions n times, where n= any number
Undelete (F1)	Restores the last three deletions

Clearing the Screen

Now that you know how to move around a document and how to use several different types of editing keys, you will correct the rough draft of the welcome letter Karen created. A copy of the rough draft is in another file named LETTER2.

Before retrieving a new file, you must clear the current document from the screen. If you do not clear the current document from the screen, the file you retrieve will combine with the document on the screen, creating a third document.

All WordPerfect 5.1 commands are issued by using the pull-down menu or the function key combination. As you use WordPerfect 5.1 commands throughout this series of labs, the command will be presented using both the function keys and the pull-down menus. The pull-down menu command sequence will be presented first. It will appear following the word "Select." Each menu command in the sequence will be separated with >, and the mnemonic letter will appear boldfaced. For example, the command to retrieve a file will appear as "Select: **F**ile>**R**etrieve."

The function key equivalent command will appear below the pull-down menu command sequence. It will be preceded with >> for example, the command to retrieve a file using the function key will appear as ">> Retrieve (SHIFT) - (F10)."

As you become familiar with the program you will probably rely less on the pull-down menus to issue commands and more on the function keys. This is because the function keys accomplish the same procedure with fewer keystrokes. Always have your function key template handy, as you will find is a very helpful reminder of the key combination to use.

To clear the current document from the screen, use the pull-down menu command, File Exit, or the function key Exit (F7) command,

Select: File>Exit
>> Exit (F7)

The prompt in the status line, "Save Document? Yes (No)," is asking whether you want to save the changes you made to the current file, LETTER, in memory to the diskette. In most cases, before you clear a document from the screen, you will want to save the work you have done onto a diskette. In this way you would be able to retrieve the file again and resume work on it if needed. Notice that following the prompt WordPerfect displays the response to the prompt as "Yes." This is the default response. To respond to the prompt, you can type the appropriate letter (Y or N) or you can position the mouse pointer on the option and click the left button. Additionally, you can simply press ⏎ to accept the default response.

You do not want to save the edited version of the document. By responding "N" (No) to the prompt, the changes you made to the document file LETTER will not be saved. The original version of the file LETTER remains on the diskette unchanged. You can retrieve the file LETTER again and repeat the exercises for practice. To indicate that you do not want to save the document as it appears on the screen,

Type: N

The next prompt, "Exit WP? No (Yes)," is asking if you want to exit the WordPerfect program. This time the default response is "No." If you select Yes the screen clears, and the operating system prompt will appear in the lower left-hand corner of the display screen. You could then turn your computer off, load another program, or reload the WordPerfect 5.1 program. If you accept the default (No), the display screen will clear and you can continue using the WordPerfect 5.1 program by creating a new document or, as you will do, retrieving another document file. Since you want to continue working in WordPerfect,

Press: ⏎

The document LETTER is cleared from the screen, and a blank WordPerfect screen is displayed.

Listing File Names

The new file you want to use is named LETTER2. A listing of the files on the disk can be displayed by using the List Files or List (F5) command.

Select: File>List Files
>> List (F5)

The name of the current directory (B or A) is displayed in the status line. If you wanted to see a display of the files on a diskette in another drive, you could enter the name of the new directory. A listing of the files in that directory would then be displayed. The current drive, however, would not change. If you wanted to actually change the current directory to another directory, you would type =, as the prompt in the status line indicates. The current directory name would disappear. You could then enter the name of the directory you wanted to use. Since you simply want to see a listing of the files on the diskette in the current (A or B) drive,

Press:

Your display screen should be similar to Figure 1-30.

FIGURE 1-30

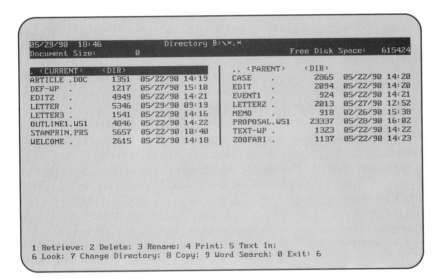

The top of the screen displays the current date and time, the name of the directory being viewed, the size of the document you are currently working on, and the remaining free diskette space. Beneath this information is an alphabetized list of the files in the directory in two columns. The file names are alphabetized from left to right across the column and then down the column. The directory includes files which are not WordPerfect files. The files listed on your screen may differ from the files in Figure 1-30 depending upon the software programs selected by your instructor.

The file you want to retrieve, LETTER2, appears in the directory. The menu of **options** in the status line allows you to organize and work with the files on the disk. An option is selected by typing the number to the left of the option name, or typing the highlighted letter, or positioning the mouse pointer on the option and clicking the left mouse button. Notice the first menu option, 1 Retrieve. By selecting this option you can retrieve the WordPerfect file you want to use. To do this, first you need to move the highlight bar, by using the arrow keys or by dragging the mouse, over the file name you want to retrieve.

Move to: LETTER2

With the highlight bar over the file name you want to retrieve, to retrieve the file,

Select: Retrieve

The document LETTER2 is displayed on the screen. Using the List Files ((F5)) command to display a file directory and retrieve a file is very helpful when you are not sure of the name of the file you want to use. The result, retrieval of a file, is the same as if you used the Retrieve ((SHIFT) - (F10)) command or selected File>Retrieve from the menu.

Editing the Welcome Letter

The rough draft of the welcome letter is displayed on the screen. Using the editing features presented above, correct the letter on your screen. Refer to Figure 1-31 for missing words. Use it as a guide to how your screen should appear when you are done. Check that there is only one blank space between words and following a period.

Saving and Replacing an Existing File

The file saved on the diskette as LETTER2 does not include the editing changes you have just made to the document on the screen. When you are entering text, it is stored temporary memory (RAM) only. Not until you **save** the document to the diskette are you safe from losing your work due to power failure or other mishap.

To save the document to disk and continue working on the file, use the File>Save or (F10) command.

Select: File>Save
   >>   Save (F10)

The prompt "Document to be saved:" is dispalyed followed by the drive and filename of the file you are currently using.

You could save both the original version of the document and the revised document as two separate files. To do this, you would enter a new file name for the revised version at this prompt. However, you do not want to keep the original version. Instead you will **replace,** or write over, it with the current version of the document on the screen. To save the current version of the document on the display screen over the version currently on the diskette, using the same file name,

Press: (⏎)

Your display screen should be similar to Figure 1-31.

FIGURE 1-31

```
Dear New Sports Club Member:

Congratulations on your new membership in the Sports Club. All of
us on the staff welcome you and encourage you to participate in
the many tournaments, leagues and club activities offered
throughout the year.

Each month you will receive a newsletter about the upcoming
events at the club. If you have questions about the event or
would like to sign up to participate in an event, just call or
come in to the front desk personnel.

The club facilities include 18 lighted tennis courts, 5
racquetball courts, an olympic size swimming pool, Nautilus
equipped weight room, and basketball court. For your comfort
while using the club, the men's and ladies' locker rooms each
have showers, a sauna, and a steam room. A spa for both men and
women is located between the locker rooms. The lounge and cafe
are open to serve you throughout the day and evening.

On behalf of the staff of the Sports Club, I hope your
association with the Club is long and enjoyable.


Replace B:\LETTER2? No (Yes)
```

The next prompt , "Replace!," protects the user from accidentally writing over an existing file. It asks you to confirm that you want to replace the contents of the file on the diskette with the revised document on the display.

If you enter N (No), the "Document to be Saved:" prompt appears again to allow you to enter a new file name. Since you want to replace the original document on the diskette with the new document on the display,

Type: **Y**

The revised document writes over the original document saved on the diskette, and you are returned to the document.

Printing a Document

Karen wants to print a hard copy of the welcome letter to give to the Membership Coordinator. If you have printer capability you can print a copy of the document displayed on the screen.

Note: Please consult your instructor for printing procedures that may differ from the directions below.

The Print menu is accessed by selecting Print from the File menu or by pressing (SHIFT) - (F7) (Print).

Select: File>Print
     >>   Print (SHIFT) - (F7)

Your display screen should be similar to Figure 1-32.

FIGURE 1-32

```
Print

     1 - Full Document
     2 - Page
     3 - Document on Disk
     4 - Control Printer
     5 - Multiple Pages
     6 - View Document
     7 - Initialize Printer


Options

     S - Select Printer                  Standard Printer
     B - Binding Offset                  0"
     N - Number of Copies                1
     U - Multiple Copies Generated by    WordPerfect
     G - Graphics Quality                Medium
     T - Text Quality                    Draft



Selection: 0
```

The document has been temporarily removed from the screen to display the Print screen. This screen is divided into two menus, Print and Options. The Print menu lets you print a document from the screen or from a document stored on a disk. The Options menu lets you select the printer and make changes to the printer settings.

In the Options menu, notice that to the right of the menu options, the selected printer and printer settings are displayed. The selected printer is Standard Printer. This is the **active printer**, or the printer that WordPerfect 5.1 expects to use to print the document.

The active printer can be changed using the Select Printer option.

Select: Select Printer

The Select Printer screen is displayed. At the top of the screen is a list of printers your school has defined. If Standard Printer is listed here, it will be highlighted, and an asterisk (*) indicates that it is the active printer.

To select the appropriate printer, first move the highlight bar to the name of the printer you want to use. The Select option (1) in the menu in the status line lets you change the highlighted printer to the active printer.

Select: Select

You are returned to the Print screen, and the printer you selected should be displayed as the active printer.

Now you are ready to instruct WordPerfect to print the letter. If necessary turn the printer on and adjust the paper so that the perforation is just above the printer scale.

The first two Print menu options let you specify how much of the document you want printed. If you wanted to print the full document, then option 1 Full Document would be selected. If you wanted to print only the page the cursor is on, then you would select **P**age.

To print a copy of the entire document,

Select: Full Document

Your printer should be printing out the document, and the letter is again displayed on your screen.

The printed copy of the welcome letter should be similar to Figure 1-33. It may not match exactly if you changed the active printer from Standard Printer to another printer. The number of words on a line in your printed document and the document on your screen may have changed. This is a result of the printer you selected.

FIGURE 1-33

```
Dear New Sports Club Member:

Congratulations on your new membership in the Sports Club. All of
us on the staff welcome you and encourage you to participate in
the many tournaments, leagues and club activities offered
throughout the year.

Each month you will receive a newsletter about the upcoming
events at the club. If you have questions about the event or
would like to sign up to participate in an event, just call or
come in to the front desk personnel.

The club facilities include 18 lighted tennis courts, 5
racquetball courts, an olympic size swimming pool, Nautilus
equipped weight room, and basketball court. For your comfort
while using the club, the men's and ladies' locker rooms each
have showers, a sauna, and a steam room. A spa for both men and
women is located between the locker rooms. The lounge and cafe
are open to serve you throughout the day and evening.

On behalf of the staff of the Sports Club, I hope your
association with the Club is long and enjoyable.

Sincerely,


Sports Club Manager
```

Notice that the right margins are even, rather than uneven or **ragged** as shown on the screen. This is one of WordPerfect's default print settings. You will look at several of these settings in the next lab.

Note: Documents created with WordPerfect 5.1 are printer-specific. That is, documents specify the active printer. All the document files supplied with the labs specify the Standard Printer as the active printer. To print any of these files, you may need to change the active printer to one appropriate for your particular microcomputer system.

Exiting WordPerfect 5.1

To leave WordPerfect 5.1 select File>Exit or Exit (F7).

Select: File>Exit
>> Exit (F7)

In response to the prompt to save the file, you can respond No, since no changes were made to the document since you last saved it.

Select: No

To exit WordPerfect 5.1,

Select: Yes

You are returned to the DOS prompt.

Always exit the WordPerfect 5.1 program using the File>Exit ((F7)) command. Never turn off your computer until you exit properly, or you may lose text.

KEY TERMS

cursor   scroll
status line   edit
document   delete
window   reformat
page   Insert mode
line   Typeover mode
position   repeater
default   hard carriage return
pull-down menu   buffer
menu bar   option
menu cursor   replace
submenu   save
mnemonic letter   active printer
prompt   ragged
context-sensitive

MATCHING

1. (F7)   _____ a. displays a menu of command choices that can be selected

2. (ESC)   _____ b. cancels a command or exits a file

3. typeover   _____ c. a question or indicator from the program that requires input from the user

4. status line   _____ d. new text writes over old text in a document

5. (ALT) - =   _____ e. creates a hard carriage return

6. prompt   _____   **f.**   retrieves a document file

7. ⟨⏎⟩   _____   **g.**   deletes word cursor is on

8. ⟨SHIFT⟩ - ⟨F10⟩   _____   **h.**   displays cursor location information or menu and command prompts

9. ⟨CTRL⟩ - ⟨BKSP⟩   _____   **i.**   deletes several lines of text

10. ⟨ESC⟩ ⟨CTRL⟩ - ⟨END⟩   _____   **j.**   causes a command to repeat a specified number of times

PRACTICE EXERCISES

1. Retrieve the file QUOTE. This file consists of a series of quotes that contain many typing errors. Follow the directions in the file to correct the sentences. Save the edited version of the file as QUOTE. Print a copy of the edited document. Remember to select the appropriate printer for your microcomputer system.

Assignment

2. Retrieve the file BUSCOMM. This file contains information related to professional communications. Follow the directions above the paragraphs to correct the text in this file. Save the edited file as BUSCOMM. Print a copy of the file. Remember to select the appropriate printer for your microcomputer system.

A A

3. Retrieve the file SPEAKING. This file is about why many people are afraid of public speaking. Edit the document, using the commands you learned in this lab. Save the edited file as SPEAKING. Print a copy of the edited document. Remember to select the appropriate printer for your microcomputer system.

SP

4. Retrieve the file INTRVIEW. This file explains how to prepare yourself for an interview. Correct the text in this file, using the commands you have learned in this lab. Save the corrected version of the file as INTRVIEW. Print the edited document. Remember to select the appropriate printer for your microcomputer system.

int

WORD PROCESSING

Creating and Formatting a Document

2

CASE STUDY

After editing the rough draft of the welcome letter, Karen showed it to the membership coordinator. The coordinator would like the letter to include information about monthly club fees and the new automatic fee payment program. We will follow Karen as she enters the new information into a file, combines it with the welcome letter, and adds some finishing touches to the letter.

Creating a Document

Boot the system by turning on the computer and loading DOS. Enter the current date when responding to the DOS date prompt. Load WordPerfect. If you are not sure of the procedure, refer to Lab 1, "Introduction to WordPerfect."

A blank WordPerfect screen is like a blank piece of paper you put into the typewriter. To create a new document, simply begin typing the text. When the cursor reaches the end of a line, however, do not press ⏎. WordPerfect will decide when to move the words down to next line based on the margin settings. This is called **word wrap**. The only time you need to press ⏎ is at the end of a paragraph or to insert blank lines.

As you type the text shown below, do not press ⏎ until you are directed to at the end of the paragraph. There should be one space following a period at the end of a sentence. If you make typing errors as you enter the text, use the editing features you learned in Lab 1 to correct your errors.

Type: The Sports Club is offering a new program to all its members which will save you writing a check each month. Upon your authorization, the bank will send payment of your monthly charges directly to the club. You will receive a copy of your monthly statement to confirm the accuracy of your bill. If you are interested in the automatic fee payment program, please contact the accounting department to make the necessary arrangements (931-4285 ext. 33).

Press:

Your display screen should be similar to Figure 2-1.

FIGURE 2-1

```
The Sports Club is offering a new program to all its members
which will save you writing a check each month. Upon your
authorization, the bank will send payment of your monthly charges
directly to the club. You will receive a copy of your monthly
statement to confirm the accuracy of your bill. If you are
interested in the automatic fee payment program, please contact
the accounting department to make the necessary arrangements
(931-4285 ext. 33)._




                                    Doc 1 Pg 1 Ln 2.17" Pos 2.8"
```

The text on your screen may not exactly match the text in Figure 2-1. This is because the active printer your WordPerfect 5.1 program is using controls the font (print) size, which affects the number of characters WordPerfect can display on a line and where it will word wrap the line of text.

As you can see, the automatic word wrap feature makes entering text in a document much faster than typing. This is because a carriage return does not need to be pressed at the end of every line.

To insert a blank line,

Press:

To enter the second paragraph,

Type: The regular monthly membership fee is $45.00. Other expenses, such as league and lesson fees, pro-shop purchases, and charges at the Courtside Cafe can also be billed to your account. The charges will be itemized on your monthly statement and added to your regular monthly fee.

To end the second paragraph,

Press: ⮐

Your display screen should be similar to Figure 2-2.

FIGURE 2-2

```
The Sports Club is offering a new program to all its members
which will save you writing a check each month. Upon your
authorization, the bank will send payment of your monthly charges
directly to the club. You will receive a copy of your monthly
statement to confirm the accuracy of your bill. If you are
interested in the automatic fee payment program, please contact
the accounting department to make the necessary arrangements
(931-4285 ext. 33).

The regular monthly membership fee is $45.00. Other expenses,
such as league and lesson fees, pro-shop purchases, and charges
at the Courtside Cafe can also be billed to your account. The
charges will be itemized on your monthly statement and added to
your regular monthly fee.
_
                                            Doc 1 Pg 1 Ln 3.33" Pos 1"
```

Check that you have entered the two paragraphs correctly. Do not be concerned if there is a difference in where WordPerfect decided to word wrap. If you find any errors, correct them using the editing features you learned in Lab 1.

Spell-Checking

It is always a good idea to check your spelling in a document when you are finished working on it. To help you do this quickly, WordPerfect has a built-in dictionary that checks for spelling errors. Additionally it will look for words which are incorrectly capitalized and duplicate words.

To enter several intentional errors in this document,

Change the spelling of "Sports" to "Sprots" in the first line.
Enter a second "new" after the word "new" in the first line.
Change the word "program" to "pROgram" in the first line.

Now you will check the spelling of your document. If you are running WordPerfect from a two-disk system, remove your data disk from drive B and insert the Speller disk. If you have a hard-disk system, WordPerfect will automatically access the spell-check program on your disk.

Begin by positioning the cursor at the top of the document so that the entire document will be checked.

Press: PGUP

To begin spell-checking,

Select: **T**ools>Spell
    >>   Spell (CTRL) - (F2)

The menu in the status line lets you specify how much of the document you want to check. You can spell-check a word, a page, or a whole document. To check the document,

Select: **D**ocument

Your screen should be similar to Figure 2-3.

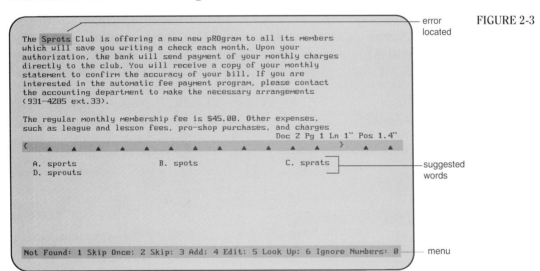

FIGURE 2-3

The Speller has encountered the first word which is not in its dictionary. The word "Sprots" is highlighted. The lower half of the screen lists four suggested replacements. The menu options in the status line have the following effect:

Skip Once   accepts the word as correct for this occurrence only

Skip   accepts the word as correct throughout the spell-check of this document

Add Word   adds the word to the **supplementary dictionary**. The Speller uses the supplementary dictionary as a secondary dictionary whenever it does not encounter the word in the main dictionary. When a word is added to the supplemental dictionary, the Speller will always accept the added word as correct.

Edit   positions the cursor on the word so you can change the spelling directly

Look Up   looks up words that match a pattern

Ignore Numbers   does not check the spelling of words containing numbers

To change the spelling of the word to one of the suggested spellings, press the letter corresponding to the correct word in the list.

Press: **A**

The Speller replaces the misspelled word with the selected replacement and moves on to locate the next error. The double word error has been located. The menu options in the status line have the following effect:

Skip	leaves the words as they are
Delete 2nd	deletes the second occurrence of the word
Edit	positions the cursor on the second duplicate word so you can edit it
Disable Double Word Checking	ignores double-occurring words for the rest of the document

To delete the second duplicate word,

Select: **3** Delete 2nd

The next error the Speller locates is the capitalization error. To edit the word,

Select: **4** Edit

Correct the word to "program."
To resume spell-checking,

Press: Exit (F7)

Finally the Speller stops on the word "Courtside." Although this is the correct spelling for the word, the Speller dictionary does not contain this word. To leave the word as it is in the document,

Select: **2** Skip

There should be no other misspelled words. However, if the speller encounters others in your file, correct them as needed. When no others are located the word count is displayed. To exit the spell-checker,

Press: Space bar

Note for two-disk users: Remove the Speller disk from drive B and insert your data disk.

Saving a New File

Next Karen needs to retrieve the file containing the welcome letter and add the new paragraphs to it. But first she needs to save the current document to the diskette and clear the screen.

You could use the File>Save or (F10) command to save the revised document. But as you saw in the previous lab, this command returns you to the document. Since Karen does not want to keep working on the same file, she will save the file while clearing the screen by using the File>Exit or (F7) command.

The difference between the Save command and the Exit command is:

Save   saves the document on the diskette and returns you to the current document.

Exit   saves the document on the diskette, clears the document from the screen (and memory), and lets you either continue working with WordPerfect by retrieving or creating another document, or leave the program.

To save the two paragraphs on the screen to a file on the diskette, use the File>Exit or (F7) command.

Select: **File>Exit**
      >>   **Exit (F7)**

The prompt "Document to be saved:" appears in the status line. WordPerfect is prompting you to enter the name of the file. The file name should be descriptive of the contents of the file. It can consist of two parts.

The first part of the file name is required and can be up to eight characters long. There can be no spaces within it. If you want to use two words in the name, separate them with a hyphen or an underscore. You will use the file name AUTO-PAY.

The second part of the file name is the file extension. It can be up to three characters long and is separated from the first part of the file name by a period. It is not required. You will use the extension .DOC to show that this is a document file. The file name can be entered in either upper- or lowercase letters.

Type: **AUTO-PAY.DOC**
Press: ⏎

After a few moments the document is saved on the diskette and cleared from the screen. At this point you could leave the WordPerfect program by entering **Y** to the prompt, "Exit WP?." However, since you have a lot more to do, in response to the prompt,

Type: **N**

Next Karen will retrieve the welcome letter. A complete, corrected copy of the welcome letter is saved for you in a file named LETTER3.

Retrieve the file LETTER3 using either File>Retrieve (SHIFT) - (F10) or File>List Files (F5).

WORD PROCESSING

Combining Files

The welcome letter is displayed on the screen. After looking at the letter Karen decides she wants the two new paragraphs from the AUTO-PAY.DOC file to be entered following the third paragraph of the welcome letter.

Move to: Ln 4.17" Pos 1" (beginning of blank line separating paragraphs three and four)

The contents of two files can be combined easily be retrieving the second file without clearing the display screen of the current file. A copy of the contents of the retrieved file is entered at the location of the cursor into the document on the display screen.

To combine the text in the AUTO-PAY.DOC file with the current file (LET-TER3) on the display, at the location of the cursor, retrieve the AUTO-PAY.DOC file using either File>Retrieve (SHIFT) - (F10) or File>List Files (F5). If you use List Files, respond Yes to the prompt in the status line to combine with the current document.

Your display screen should be similar to Figure 2-4.

FIGURE 2-4

```
Dear New Sports Club Member:

Congratulations on your new membership in the Sports Club. All of
us on the staff welcome you and encourage you to participate in
the many tournaments, leagues and club activities offered
throughout the year.

Each month you will receive a newsletter about the upcoming
events at the club. If you have questions about the event or
would like to sign up to participate in an event, just call or
come in to the front desk personnel.

The club facilities include 18 lighted tennis courts, 5
racquetball courts, an olympic size swimming pool, Nautilus
equipped weight room, and basketball court. For your comfort
while using the club, the men's and ladies' locker rooms each
have showers, a sauna, and a steam room. A spa for both men and
women is located between the locker rooms. The lounge and cafe
are open to serve you throughout the day and evening.
The Sports Club is offering a new program to all its members
which will save you writing a check each month. Upon your
authorization, the bank will send payment of your monthly charges
directly to the club. You will receive a copy of your monthly
statement to confirm the accuracy of your bill. If you are
B:\LETTER3                                    Doc 1 Pg 1 Ln 4.17" Pos 1"
```

AUTO-PAY.DOC text
combined with LETTER3

The two paragraphs from the AUTO-PAY.DOC file have been inserted into the welcome letter at the location of the cursor.

To separate paragraphs 3 and 4 with a blank line,

Press: (⏎)

To view the rest of the text, using the (↓) key,

Move to: Ln 8.17" Pos 1" (last line of letter)

Moving Text

After looking over the welcome letter Karen decides she would like to change the order of the paragraphs in the letter. She wants the paragraph about the automatic fee payment program (paragraph 4) to follow the paragraph about the monthly membership fees (paragraph 5).

A complete sentence, paragraph, or page of text can be moved by selecting Edit>Select from the menu or by using the Move (CTRL) - (F4) command. First the cursor must be positioned anywhere within the piece of text to be moved. You will place the cursor on the first character (T) of paragraph 4.

Move to: Ln 4.33" Pos 1" ("T" of "The" at beginning of paragraph 4)

Next, to use the pull-down menu to select the Move command,

Select: Edit>Select

There are three submenu options available for selection: Sentence, Paragraph, and Page. These options allow you to specify the area of text to be moved. To specify a paragraph,

Select: Paragraph

Your display screen should be similar to Figure 2-5.

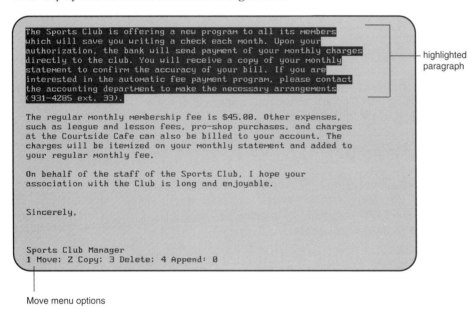

FIGURE 2-5

highlighted paragraph

Move menu options

The entire paragraph is highlighted. Only one sentence, paragraph, or page of text can be marked (highlighted) for moving at a time.

The status line now displays four more menu options: Move, Copy, Delete, and Append. They have the following meanings:

Move   allows you to remove the text from its present location so it can be moved to another location

Copy   leaves the original text and moves a duplicate to another location

Delete   permanently removes the text from the document

Append   lets you add the text to the end of a file on the disk

The default option, 0, displayed at the end of the menu, allows you to cancel the command. A menu option which appears in the status line is selected by typing the number to the left of the option you want to use or by typing the highlighted letter. Rather than select the Move option at this time, you will cancel your command selections. This will allow you to see how the Move command works when using the function key equivalent, (CTRL) - (F4).

Press: (⏎)

To reposition the cursor within the paragraph to be moved,

Press: (↑) (2 times)

The cursor should be on Ln 5.55" Pos 1" (the "(" of the telephone number).
    To use the function key equivalent,

Press: (CTRL) - (F4)

The same three options, which let you specify the area of text to move (**S**entence, **P**aragraph, or Pa**g**e), appear in the status line.
    To specify the entire paragraph,

Select: **P**aragraph

Your screen should again look like Figure 2-5.
    Now the same menu of four Move options appears in the status line. To continue the Move command by moving the paragraph from one location in the document to another, select Move as follows:

Select: **M**ove

The marked paragraph is removed from the document and is stored in temporary memory until needed. The text below the deleted paragraph moves up. The status line now directs you to move the cursor and press (⏎) to retrieve the text.
    You will reenter the paragraph below the paragraph on the monthly fees. To do this,

Move to: Ln 5.33" Pos 1" ("O" of "On")
Press: (⏎)

Your display screen should be similar to Figure 2-6.

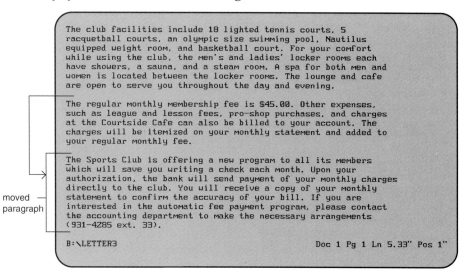

The club facilities include 18 lighted tennis courts, 5
racquetball courts, an olympic size swimming pool, Nautilus
equipped weight room, and basketball court. For your comfort
while using the club, the men's and ladies' locker rooms each
have showers, a sauna, and a steam room. A spa for both men and
women is located between the locker rooms. The lounge and cafe
are open to serve you throughout the day and evening.

The regular monthly membership fee is $45.00. Other expenses,
such as league and lesson fees, pro-shop purchases, and charges
at the Courtside Cafe can also be billed to your account. The
charges will be itemized on your monthly statement and added to
your regular monthly fee.

The Sports Club is offering a new program to all its members
which will save you writing a check each month. Upon your
authorization, the bank will send payment of your monthly charges
directly to the club. You will receive a copy of your monthly
statement to confirm the accuracy of your bill. If you are
interested in the automatic fee payment program, please contact
the accounting department to make the necessary arrangements
(931-4285 ext. 33).

moved —
paragraph

B:\LETTER3   Doc 1 Pg 1 Ln 5.33" Pos 1"

FIGURE 2-6

The marked paragraph is reentered into the document beginning at the cursor location. That was a lot quicker than retyping the whole paragraph!

Note: When the use of the function key command instruction requires a selection from a menu displayed in the status line, the instructions will appear separated by commas. For example: >> (CTRL) - (F4), **2 P**aragraph, **1 M**ove.

Using the Block Command

Next Karen wants to move the telephone number of the accounting department. She wants it to follow the reference to the accounting department in the same sentence. Because the telephone number is not a complete sentence, paragraph, or page of text, the Move command cannot be used by itself. Instead it is used along with the Block command.

The Block (Edit>Block or (ALT) - (F4)) command is used to mark an area, or **block**, of text. A block of text can be as short as a single letter or as long as several pages of text. The marked text can then be acted upon by the Move command.

Before using the Block command, the cursor must be placed on the first character in the block of text to be moved. In this case it is the opening parenthesis surrounding the telephone number.

Move to: Ln 6.5" Pos 1" ("(" at beginning of telephone number)

To access the Block command,

Select: **E**dit>**B**lock
  >>   Block (ALT) - (F4)

Note: Dragging the mouse across text automatically turns on the Block feature. Therefore, if you use the mouse to specify a block of text, you do not need to select Edit>Block or press (ALT) - (F4) first.

The message "Block on" flashes in the status line. This shows that the Block command is active. Next, the area of text to be moved must be identified. To do this the text is highlighted by moving the cursor using the cursor movement keys or dragging the mouse (hold down the left button while moving the mouse) to the end of the area of text to be moved. To highlight the telephone number, using (→) or dragging the mouse,

Move to: Ln 6.5" Pos 2.7" (")" of telephone number)

The highlight should cover the phone number through the closing parenthesis. The text to be moved is now defined. Once a block of text is defined many different WordPerfect commands can be used to manipulate the block. For example, it can be underlined, deleted, copied, or centered on the page.

Karen wants to move this block of text to another location in the document. To do this the Move (**E**dit>**M**ove or (CTRL) - (F4)) command is used.

Note: If you use (CTRL) - (F4) to issue this command you will need to select an option from the menus displayed in the status line. The three options in the first menu let you specify the type of text to be moved. Since you defined a block of text you will select **B**lock. A second menu appears which lets you tell the program what you want to do with the block. Since you want to move a block, you will select **M**ove.

Select: **E**dit>**M**ove (Cut)

   >>   Move (CTRL) - (F4), **B**lock, **M**ove

Your display screen should be similar to Figure 2-7.

FIGURE 2-7

```
The club facilities include 18 lighted tennis courts, 5
racquetball courts, an olympic size swimming pool, Nautilus
equipped weight room, and basketball court. For your comfort
while using the club, the men's and ladies' locker rooms each
have showers, a sauna, and a steam room. A spa for both men and
women is located between the locker rooms. The lounge and cafe
are open to serve you throughout the day and evening.

The regular monthly membership fee is $45.00. Other expenses,
such as league and lesson fees, pro-shop purchases, and charges
at the Courtside Cafe can also be billed to your account. The
charges will be itemized on your monthly statement and added to
your regular monthly fee.

The Sports Club is offering a new program to all its members
which will save you writing a check each month. Upon your
authorization, the bank will send payment of your monthly charges
directly to the club. You will receive a copy of your monthly
statement to confirm the accuracy of your bill. If you are
interested in the automatic fee payment program, please contact
the accounting department to make the necessary arrangements
.

─
Move cursor; press Enter to retrieve.          Doc 1 Pg 1 Ln 6.5" Pos 1"
```

The block of text is temporarily removed from the document. It will remain in temporary memory until (←) is pressed.

As long as you do not press (←) you can do other simple editing tasks before completing the Move command. For instance, notice that there is a space left before the period at the cursor location. While the cursor is positioned properly, you can delete the space before using the Move command. To delete the space,

Press: (BKSP)

You can now move the cursor to the location where you want the block to appear. Karen wants it to follow the word "department."

Move to: Ln 6.33" Pos 3.5" (blank space after "department")

You are now ready to retrieve the block. To do this,

Press: ⏎

Your display screen should be similar to Figure 2-8.

FIGURE 2-8

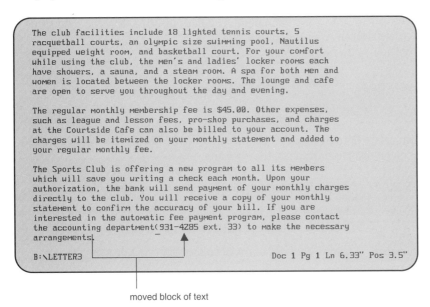

moved block of text

The telephone number for the accounting department now follows the reference to the department in the sentence.

To insert a space before the opening parenthesis of the telephone number,

Press: Space bar

After looking over the letter for a while, Karen decides she wants to make the following changes:

- enter the current date in the upper right-hand corner
- increase the margin width
- indent the first line of each paragraph
- replace the word "club" with "sports club"
- change the right margin to print ragged

You will follow Karen as she makes these changes to the Welcome letter.

Using the Date Command

Karen wants the date to be entered on the first line of the letter. To move to the top of the letter and insert a blank line,

Press: (PGUP)
Press: (⏎)
Press: (↑)

A blank line has been inserted at the top of the letter where the date will be entered.

The Date command (Tools>Date Code or Date (SHIFT) - (F5), Date Code) inserts the current date into your document. The date inserted into the document is the date you entered when responding to the DOS date prompt.

To use the Date command,

Select: Tools
>> Date (SHIFT) - (F5)

The three date options in the Tools menu (or if you use the function key command, in the menu displayed in the status line) are:

Date Text   inserts the current date as text into your document

Date Code   inserts a WordPerfect code, which automatically updates the date whenever the file is retrieved or printed

Date Format   allows changes to the default date format display

The welcome letter will be mailed to new members as they join the club. Karen wants the current date automatically entered whenever the letter is printed. To do this, the Date Code option is used.

Select: Date Code

Your display screen should be similar to Figure 2-9.

FIGURE 2-9

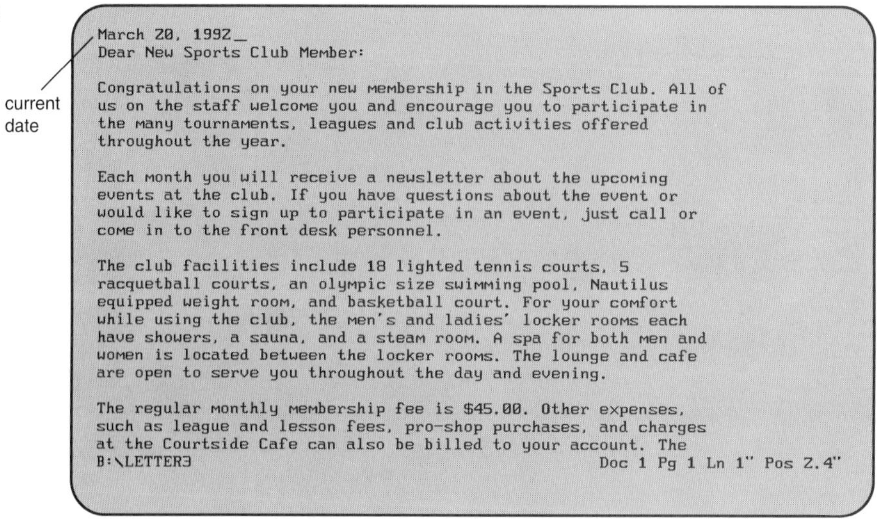

current date

The current date is entered into the letter at the location of the cursor. It appears as text, not as a WordPerfect code. Whenever this file is retrieved or printed, the current system date will be displayed using this format. You will see shortly how the date is stored as a WordPerfect code.

Note: The date in Figure 2-9 will be different from the date that appears on your display. If you did not enter the current date at the DOS prompt, then the default system date will be used.

Aligning Text Flush with the Right Margin

Next Karen wants the date to end against the right margin or to be **flush right**. The Flush Right command (Layout>Align>Flush Right or Flush Right (ALT) - (F6)) is used to do this. For this command to work correctly the cursor must first be positioned on the first character of the text to be moved and there must be a hard carriage return at the end of the existing line of text. To position the cursor at the beginning of the date,

Press: ⌐←⌐

Because the date is a WordPerfect code rather than text you entered character by character, the program considers the date a single character, and the cursor jumps quickly to Ln 1" Pos 1".

To move the date flush with the right margin and reformat the display, using the pull-down menu,

Select: Layout

The Layout menu options affect the design of the document. We will be using many of these options shortly. The Align option controls the placement of text on a line.

Select: Align

Your screen should be similar to Figure 2-10.

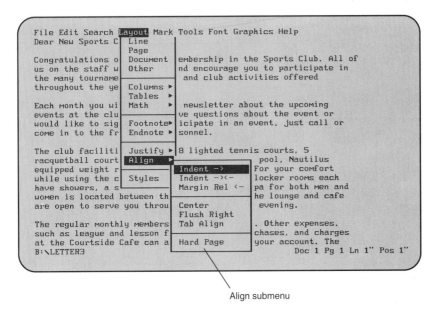

FIGURE 2-10

Align submenu

There are three submenu options which affect the placement of text on a line: Center, Flush Right, and Tab Align. To align the text located to the right of the cursor flush with the right margin,

Select: Flush Right

To reformat the display of the line,

Press: ⊕

Your display screen should be similar to Figure 2-11.

FIGURE 2-11

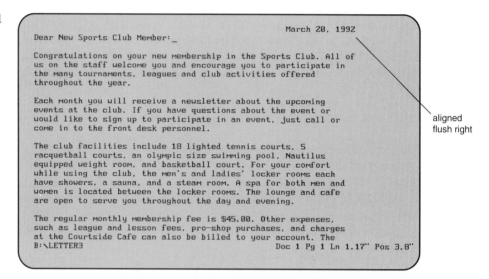

aligned
flush right

The date has moved flush with the right margin.

The function key command equivalent is simply Flush Right (ALT) - (F6). In this case, using the function key would be quicker than using the pull-down menus.

The Flush Right command can also be used before typing in new text that you want aligned with the right margin. As you type the text it is entered so that the last character in the line is even with the right margin.

Next Karen wants the date separated from the salutation by four blank lines. To move to the beginning of line 2 and insert four blank lines between the date line and the salutation,

Press: (HOME)
Press: (←)
Press: (↵) (4 times)

The salutation begins on line 1.83".

Setting Margins

Karen would like to change the right and left margin widths from 1 inch (the default setting) to 1-1/2 inches. To change the left and right margin widths of a document, the Line Format (Layout>Line or Format (SHIFT) - (F8)) command is used. The new margin setting must be entered at the beginning of the document so that the entire document below the setting will be formatted to the new margin specifications.

To position the cursor at the top of the document,

Press: (PGUP)

This time, you will use the function key command to set the margins.

Press: Format (SHIFT) - (F8)

Your display screen should be similar to Figure 2-12.

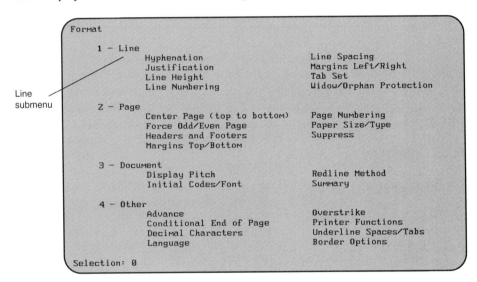

FIGURE 2-12

Line submenu

```
Format

    1 - Line
            Hyphenation                Line Spacing
            Justification             Margins Left/Right
            Line Height               Tab Set
            Line Numbering            Widow/Orphan Protection

    2 - Page
            Center Page (top to bottom)   Page Numbering
            Force Odd/Even Page            Paper Size/Type
            Headers and Footers           Suppress
            Margins Top/Bottom

    3 - Document
            Display Pitch              Redline Method
            Initial Codes/Font        Summary

    4 - Other
            Advance                   Overstrike
            Conditional End of Page   Printer Functions
            Decimal Characters        Underline Spaces/Tabs
            Language                  Border Options

Selection: 0
```

The document is replaced by a full-screen menu. This menu is divided into four submenus: 1 Line, 2 Page, 3 Document, and 4 Other. Below each submenu the options for that submenu are listed.

The Line, Page, and Other submenu options change the settings from the point they are entered into the document forward. The Document submenu options change the settings for the entire document.

The command to set margins is an option in the Line submenu.

Select: Line

Your display screen should be similar to Figure 2-13.

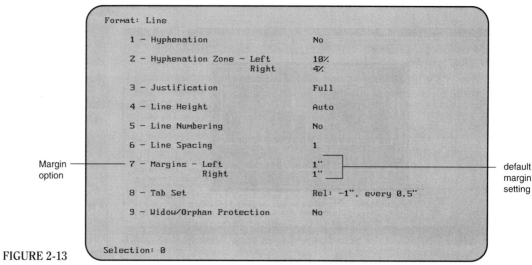

```
Format: Line

        1 - Hyphenation                      No

        2 - Hyphenation Zone - Left          10%
                              Right          4%

        3 - Justification                    Full

        4 - Line Height                      Auto

        5 - Line Numbering                   No

        6 - Line Spacing                     1

Margin  7 - Margins - Left                   1"                              default
option              Right                    1"                              margin
                                                                             setting
        8 - Tab Set                          Rel: -1", every 0.5"

        9 - Widow/Orphan Protection          No


        Selection: 0
```

FIGURE 2-13

The Line Format menu is displayed. The left side of the menu lists the 9 options which affect line endings, spacing, numbering, length, and tabs. The right column displays the current settings, in this case the default settings, for each option. The Margins option lets you specify new left and right margins. The default margin settings provide 1 inch of space from the left and right edge of the paper.

Select: **Margins**

The cursor jumps to the right column under the setting for the left margin. The margin setting can be entered as a decimal or as a fraction. To change the left margin setting to 1-1/2 inches, you could enter either 1.5 or 1 1/2.

Type: **1.5**
Press: ⏎

The cursor moves to the right margin setting. To change the right margin,

Type: **1 1/2**
Press: ⏎

WordPerfect converts the fraction to a decimal.

If you wanted you could continue to select other Line Format options. However, Karen first wants to see how the document has changed with the new margin settings. To quickly leave the Line Format menu and return directly to the document, use the Exit command, (F7).

Press: **Exit (F7)**

The left margin now begins at Pos 1.5"; however, the right margin has not adjusted to the new right margin setting. To reformat the display of text on the screen,

Press: (HOME)
Press: ⬇

Your display screen should be similar to Figure 2-14.

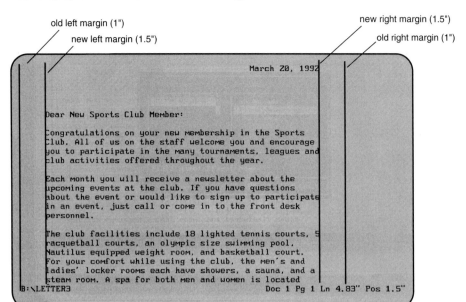

FIGURE 2-14

The letter has been reformatted to fit within the new margin settings.
To return to the top of the letter,

Press: (HOME)
Press: (↑)

Using and Setting Tabs

Next Karen wants to indent the first line of each paragraph and the closing. The **Tab** key lets you easily indent text on a line. WordPerfect has set the default tab setting at every half inch. As with other default settings, the Tab spacing can also be set to your needs. The Line Format command, (Layout>Line or (SHIFT) - (F8), Line), is used to view and set tabs.

Select: **L**ayout>**L**ine
>> Format (SHIFT) - (F8) **L**ine

The Line Format menu is displayed. To display the current tab settings,

Select: **T**ab Set

Your display screen should be similar to Figure 2-15.

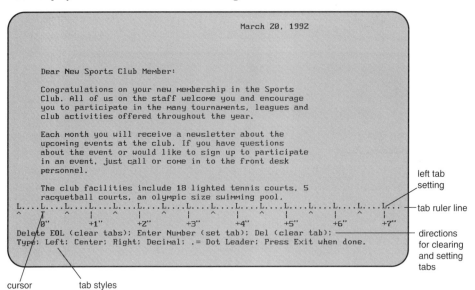

FIGURE 2-15

A Tab Ruler line is displayed at the bottom of the screen. The "L" marks the location of each tab stop from the left margin. The cursor can be moved along the ruler line using ⭢ and ⭠. For Help information about tabs,

Press: Help F3

Your screen should be similar to Figure 2-16.

FIGURE 2-16

```
Tab Set

    Sets the tab positions (tab stops) in the document.  Tab stops are
    initially set every half-inch.  To change the default, select this option.

    Tab settings in WordPerfect 5.1 are normally set relative to the left
    margin.  Press t for more information.

    You can determine how text is aligned on the tab stop (e.g., text can be
    centered).  For more information, press 1.

    You can delete the tab settings to the right of the cursor by pressing
    Delete to End of Line (Ctrl-End).  Pressing Del erases the tab setting at
    the cursor.  To set a regular tab, enter the position number (e.g. 1.75").
    To set evenly spaced tabs, enter the position for the first tab setting,
    followed by a comma and the increment measurement (e.g., 1",2" sets the
    first tab at 1", the next one at 3", etc.)

    While the cursor is located on a tab setting, you can move the tab by
    holding down Ctrl and pressing the Left or Right Arrows.  Text on the
    screen will automatically move with the new tab position.  You can move
    from tab setting to tab setting using the Alt-Arrow or Ctrl-Arrow key
    combinations as well as the Up and Down Arrows.

Selection: 0                                       (Press ENTER to exit Help)
```

After reading the information on this screen about how to clear and set tabs, following the directions on the screen to obtain more information about tab styles,

Type: 1

This information describes the four styles or types of tabs you can create using the Tab menu.

To return to the document,

Press: ⟨⏎⟩

To review, the basic procedures for clearing and setting tabs are:

- Clear an individual tab setting by placing the cursor on the tab stop and pressing (DEL).

- Clear multiple tab settings by placing the cursor on the first tab stop to be deleted and using (CTRL) - (END) to delete all tab stops from the cursor to the right.

- Enter new left tab settings by moving the cursor to the tab stop and typing L, or by entering the number.

However, Karen is satisfied with the default tab settings and does not want to make any changes. To leave the settings as they are and return to the document,

Press: Cancel (F1) (3 times)

To indent the first line of the first paragraph,

Move to: Ln 2.17" Pos 1.5" (on "C" in "Congratulations")
Press: (TAB)

Your display screen should be similar to Figure 2-17.

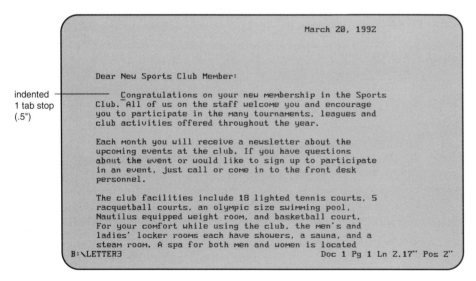

FIGURE 2-17

The first line is indented.

In a similar manner, indent the first lines of the next five paragraphs. Notice as you move down through the text that each paragraph is automatically reformatted.

To indent the closing lines,

Move to:	Ln 9.17" Pos 1.5" (on "S" in "Sincerely")
Press:	(TAB) (7 times)
Move to:	Ln 9.83" Pos 1.5" (on "S" of "Sports")
Press:	(TAB) (7 times)
Press:	ⓙ

Notice that the last line of the letter is on the last line of the page. Karen feels this does not look good and decides to reset the right and left margins back to the default setting of 1 inch.

Displaying Hidden Codes

Press: (PGUP)

Karen could reset the margins using the Line Format menu. There is another way, however, to return the margins to their original settings.

WordPerfect places hidden **codes** in the document whenever a feature is used that controls the format and display of the document. The codes consist of symbols that tell WordPerfect and the printer what to do. When the program reads the code, it reformats all the text in the document from that point on to the new setting. The codes are hidden so that your document on the display screen looks as close as possible to the text as it will appear when printed. Because the codes are hidden, your display is not cluttered.

The code is entered into the document at the location of the cursor when the command is issued. WordPerfect lets you see the hidden codes in the document so that you can remove the codes you no longer want or need. To see the hidden codes, use the Reveal Codes command (Edit>Reveal Codes or Reveal Codes (ALT) - (F3)).

Select:	**E**dit>**R**eveal Codes
>>	Reveal Codes (ALT) - (F3)

Your display screen should be similar to Figure 2-18.

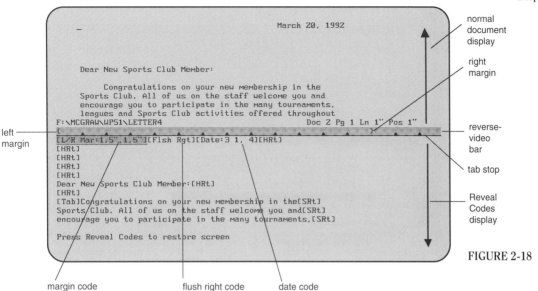

normal
document
display

right
margin

reverse-
video
bar

tab stop

Reveal
Codes
display

left
margin

FIGURE 2-18

margin code   flush right code   date code

WORD PROCESSING

The screen is divided into two windows by a reverse-video bar, which shows the left ({) and right (}) margins and tab (^) settings. The upper window displays the document as it normally appears. The lower window displays the same text with the hidden codes revealed. This is the Reveal Codes screen. The codes are always displayed in brackets ([]).

The first code displayed in the Reveal Codes screen is [L/R Mar: 1.5",1.5"]. This code controls the left and right margin settings. The first part of the code is an abbreviation of the command used. The selected settings are displayed next. Since the cursor is on this code, it is highlighted.

The next code [Flsh Rgt] is the Flush Right code which aligns the date flush with the right margin. The code [Date:3 1, 4] tells the program to enter the current date into the document. The last code [HRt] stands for a hard carriage return. This code is entered whenever you press ⏎ .

To delete a code, the (BKSP) or (DEL) key is used. The (BKSP) key will delete codes to the left of the cursor, and the (DEL) key will delete codes the cursor is highlighting.

Karen wants to delete the margin code. Since this code is highlighted, to remove it,

Press: (DEL)

Your display screen should be similar to Figure 2-19.

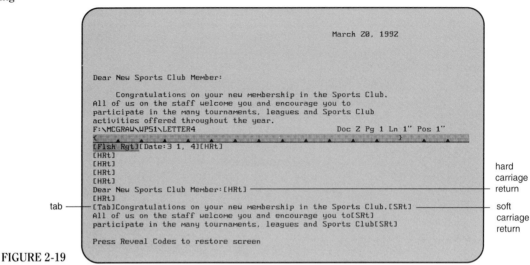

FIGURE 2-19

The code is deleted from the document. When a code is deleted, the document acts as if the code had never been entered. The removal of the margin code causes the margin settings to return to the default settings of one inch. Look in the upper window and you can see that the text is now displayed using the new margin settings.

A code also can be deleted from the document while you are in normal document display mode. That is, you do not have to use the Reveal Codes screen to remove codes. However, if you have forgotten where the code was entered in the text, then it is best to use the Reveal Codes screen while deleting codes. In either display mode, first move the cursor to the location of the code in the document. Then use (BKSP) to delete codes to the left of the cursor and (DEL) to delete codes the cursor is highlighting.

Let's look at the other codes displayed in the Reveal Codes screen. Each of the blank lines between the date and salutation is coded with the [HRt] symbol. The code that tells WordPerfect to indent the paragraph is [Tab]. At the end of each line of the first paragraph a [SRt] code is displayed. This code identifies the location of a **soft carriage return**. As WordPerfect reformats the text on the screen, it enters a [SRt] code at the end of a line. This code shows the location where WordPerfect decided to automatically word wrap to the next line.

When the Reveal Codes screen is in use you can type characters or use any WordPerfect features. The text in the Reveal Codes screen may not wrap the same as the text in the document Editing screen, however. This is because it contains the format codes.

To return to normal document display and hide the codes again, you must reselect the Reveal Codes command. To do this quickly using the function key command,

Press: Reveal Codes (ALT) - (F3)

To see where the letter ends on the page,

Press: (HOME) (HOME) (↓)

As you can see, because the margin widths were decreased, more text can be displayed on a line. Consequently, the last line of the letter is now on Ln 9".

Press: (PGUP)

Searching and Replacing Text

Next Karen wants to find all occurrences of the word "club" in the letter and change it to "Sports Club" where appropriate. The Replace (Search>Replace or Replace (ALT) - (F2)) command will help do this quickly. You will use the pull-down menu to perform this task.

Select: Search

Your screen should be similar to Figure 2-20.

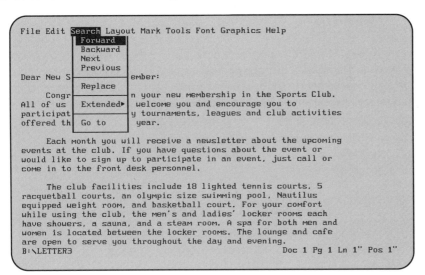

FIGURE 2-20

WordPerfect has several commands for **searching** through a file to find a **string**, or specific combination of characters and/or codes. The first two Search menu options, Forward and Backward, move the cursor either forward or backward through the document to locate the first occurrence of the combination of letters, characters or numbers specified. The function key equivalent to the Search>Forward command is Search (F2), and for the Search>Backward command it is Search (SHIFT) - (F2).

The second two options, Next and Previous, tell the program to continue the search by moving to the next occurrence or to the previous occurrence of the matching string.

The next Search menu option, Replace, moves the cursor forward through a document to locate the specified string and replaces it with another. You cannot use Replace to search backward through the text.

Replace is the command Karen wants to use.

Select: **R**eplace

The prompt "W/Confirm? No (Yes)" is displayed in the status line. If you respond **Yes** to the prompt, WordPerfect will display the matching string and ask for confirmation before replacing it. If you respond **No**, WordPerfect will automatically replace every occurrence of the word with the new string.

To selectively replace the word,

Type: Y

The "—> Srch:" prompt is displayed on the status line. The word or phrase you want to find is entered following the prompt. When entering the search string, lowercase letters will match both upper- and lowercase letters in the text. However, if you enter the search string in uppercase letters, only uppercase matches will be found. After entering the search string, do not press ⏎.

Type: club

Next, to search forward in the document,

Press: Search (F2)

The prompt "Replace with" is displayed next. If no replacement string were entered at this prompt, the word "club" would be deleted at every occurrence. You want to replace "club" with "Sports Club." The replacement string must be entered exactly as you want it to appear in your document. Do not press ⏎ after typing the replace string.

Type: **Sports Club**
Press: Search (F2)

Your display screen should be similar to Figure 2-21.

FIGURE 2-21

```
                                                    March 20, 1992

                                                                      ─ matching
                                                                        word
Dear New Sports Club Member:

    Congratulations on your new membership in the Sports Club.
All of us on the staff welcome you and encourage you to
participate in the many tournaments, leagues and club activities
offered throughout the year.

    Each month you will receive a newsletter about the upcoming
events at the club. If you have questions about the event or
would like to sign up to participate in an event, just call or
come in to the front desk personnel.

    The club facilities include 18 lighted tennis courts, 5
racquetball courts, an olympic size swimming pool, Nautilus
equipped weight room, and basketball court. For your comfort
while using the club, the men's and ladies' locker rooms each
have showers, a sauna, and a steam room. A spa for both men and
women is located between the locker rooms. The lounge and cafe
are open to serve you throughout the day and evening.
Confirm? No (Yes)
```

prompt

Immediately the cursor moves to the first word matching the search string "club." Notice that the cursor is positioned on "Club." This is because the search string was entered in all lowercase letters, and WordPerfect does not distinguish between upper- and lowercase letters when searching the text for matching strings.

The prompt "Confirm? No (Yes)" is displayed in the Status line. The first occurrence is acceptable as it is (you do not want to replace it),

Type: N (or press ⏎)

The cursor skips to the next occurrence of the word "club" and waits for your response. Again, it is already correct.

Type: N

The cursor moves to the third occurrence of the word "club" and waits for your response. This time Karen wants to replace it with "Sports Club."

Type: Y

The word "club" is replaced with the word "Sports Club." The cursor moves to the next match.
Respond to the remaining prompts to replace "club" with "Sports Club" when needed. When no more matches are located the search ends.

Setting Justification

On the screen the welcome letter has even left margins and uneven, or ragged right, margins. But, as you noted at the end of Lab 1, when the letter is printed the text is aligned evenly with both the left and right margin settings. This is called **justification**. To justify text, WordPerfect inserts extra spaces between some of the words on a line to force the line to end even with the right margin setting. Printing a document so that the text aligns against the right and left margins is the default setting in WordPerfect.

Karen wants the welcome letter to be printed with ragged right margins (as it is displayed on the screen). The command to change justification is on the Line Format menu (Layout>Line or Format (SHIFT) - (F8), Line). Using this command inserts a code in the document to control the printing of the text. The code should be entered at the beginning of the document so that the entire letter will be printed with a ragged right margin. If it is not entered at the beginning of the document, the new justification setting will begin at the cursor location and will continue until you insert another code that changes the setting.

To move the cursor to the beginning of the welcome letter and to display the Line Format menu,

Press: (PGUP)
Select: Layout>Line
   >>   Format (SHIFT) - (F8), Line

The default justification setting is Full, meaning that both the left and right margins are aligned or justified.

Select: Justification

The Justify menu at the bottom of the screen displays four justification settings. They have the following effect:

Left   aligns text against left margin, leaving right margin ragged
Center   centers each line of text between the left and right margins
Right   aligns text against right margin, leaving left margin ragged
Full   aligns text against the right and left margins

To change justification to have even left margins and ragged right margins,

Select: Left

The new justification setting "Left" is displayed in the Format Line menu.
To quickly exit the Format Line menu and return to the document,

Press: Exit (F7)

Nothing looks different on the screen. But when the document is printed the right margin will be uneven, as it is displayed.

Note: The pull-down menu option, Layout>Justify, also lets you set the justification of text in your document. It has the same four choices and produces the same effect as using Layout>Line>Justify.

Printing the Document

To print a copy of the welcome letter,

Select: File>Print
     >>   Print (SHIFT) - (F7)

The Print menu is displayed.
Let's take a moment to look at the Print options you have not used yet. The second option, Binding Offset, allows you to move the printed document to the right or left side of the paper to allow space for binding. The current setting of 0" is the default. The third option, Number of Copies, allows you to print multiple copies of a document. The default is to print 1 copy. The fourth option, Multiple Copies Generated by, is an option used by some laser printers to print more than one copy of the current print job. The default (1) lets WordPerfect control the number of copies. The last two options, Graphics Quality and Text Quality, allow you to set the quality level at which the graphics or text are printed. The lower quality settings produce a "rough" copy and print faster. The default settings for these options are displayed in the right column.
If necessary, use the Select Printer option to select the printer which is appropriate for your computer system.
To print the letter Karen could select either Full Text or Page from the Print menu, since the welcome letter is only one page long. If the text were longer than a single page, selecting Page would print only the page the cursor is positioned on.

Select: Page

Your printed letter should be similar to Figure 2-22.

FIGURE 2-22

```
                                          March 20, 1992


Dear New Sports Club Member:

      Congratulations on your new membership in the Sports Club.
All of us on the staff welcome you and encourage you to
participate in the many tournaments, leagues and Sports Club
activities offered throughout the year.

      Each month you will receive a newsletter about the upcoming
events at the Sports Club. If you have questions about the event
or would like to sign up to participate in an event, just call or
come in to the front desk personnel.

      The Sports Club facilities include 18 lighted tennis courts,
5 racquetball courts, an olympic size swimming pool, Nautilus
equipped weight room, and basketball court. For your comfort
while using the Sports Club, the men's and ladies' locker rooms
each have showers, a sauna, and a steam room. A spa for both men
and women is located between the locker rooms. The lounge and
cafe are open to serve you throughout the day and evening.

      The regular monthly membership fee is $45.00. Other
expenses, such as league and lesson fees, pro-shop purchases, and
charges at the Courtside Cafe can also be billed to your account.
The charges will be itemized on your monthly statement and added
to your regular monthly fee.

      The Sports Club is offering a new program to all its members
which will save you writing a check each month. Upon your
authorization, the bank will send payment of your monthly charges
directly to the Sports Club. You will receive a copy of your
monthly statement to confirm the accuracy of your bill. If you
are interested in the automatic fee payment program, please
contact the accounting department (931-4285 ext. 33) to make the
necessary arrangements.

      On behalf of the staff of the Sports Club, I hope your
association with the Sports Club is long and enjoyable.

                              Sincerely,



                              Sports Club Manager
```

WORD PROCESSING

Saving the Document in a New File

Karen would like to save the edited version of the welcome letter that is displayed on the screen in a new file named LETTER4. This will allow the original file, LETTER3, to remain unchanged on the diskette in case you would like to repeat the lab for practice. She is also ready to exit the WordPerfect program. To both save the document and exit the program, use the **F**ile>**Ex**it (Exit (F7)) command.

Select: **F**ile>**Ex**it
>> Exit (F7)

To respond Yes to the prompt to save the document,

Press: ⏎

To enter the new file name following the "Document to be Saved:" prompt,

Type: LETTER4
Press: ⏎

 The revised letter has been saved on the disk as LETTER4. The printer specifications which were active when the file was saved were also saved with this file. If you were to retrieve this file again, the printer you made active would appear on the Print screen as the selected printer.
 To indicate you are ready to exit the WordPerfect program,

Type: Y

KEY TERMS

word wrap
supplementary dictionary
block
flush right
code

soft carriage return
search
string
justification

MATCHING

1. word wrap — a. saves file and resumes edit
2. (F10) — b. automatic adjustment of words on a line
3. [HRt] — c. displays the Line Format menu
4. (CTRL)-(F4) — d. turns on the Block feature
5. (ALT)-(F6) — e. moves the cursor a set number of spaces
6. (SHIFT)-(F5) — f. displays the Date menu
7. margin — g. hidden code for hard carriage return
8. (TAB) — h. displays the Move menu
9. (SHIFT)-(F8) — i. border of white space around the printed document
10. (ALT)-(F4) — j. moves text flush with the right margin

PRACTICE EXERCISES

1. You are taking a class in meteorology and have to present a brief description of cloud formations to the class. You have prepared the text for your talk and saved it

in a file named CLOUDS. Retrieve the file CLOUDS. The file still needs some refinements. Follow the steps below to fix the document.

Test

a.   Set the justification to left.

b.   Move the cursor to the end of the document.

c.   Combine the text in the file CLDCLASS (on your data diskette) with the existing document CLOUDS. There should be a blank line between all the paragraphs.

d.   Indent the first line of each paragraph one tab stop.

e.   Change the order of the numbered paragraphs so that they are in numerical order. Insert a blank line between each of the numbered paragraphs.

f.   Move the three numbered paragraphs to the line directly after the paragraph beginning with "Clouds are classified on the basis of their appearance and height."

g.   Add one blank line after the last paragraph. Enter the current date using the Date command. Enter your name on the last line of the document.

h.   Spell-check the document.

i.   Save and replace this document as CLOUDS.RPT on your data diskette. Print the document.

2.   You have been asked to write an article for the Electric Company newsletter about severe weather conditions. Retrieve the file THUNDER. You need to make several modifications to your file. Follow the steps below to fix the document.

a.   Set the justification to left.

b.   Using the Edit>Select command, delete the first paragraph.

c.   Combine the file TWISTER (on your data diskette) with the current file.

d.   Find and replace all occurrences of the word "twister" with "tornado."

e.   Combine the file HURRICAN (on your data diskette) with the current file. The text in this file should be inserted below the existing text.

f.   Insert a blank line between all the paragraphs, and indent the first line of each paragraph one tab stop.

g.   Enter your name on line 1, and use the Date command to enter the current date on line 2. Leave one blank line below the date.

h.   Spell-check the document. Save the file as WEATHER. Print the completed document.

3.   You are employed by the Future Publication Company and are working on a letter to send to possible subscribers of your company's magazines. The letter still needs some work.

a.   To see the existing letter, retrieve the file SUBSCRIP.

b.   Set new margin settings of left = 1.2" and right = 1.2". Clear the existing tab settings and enter left tabs at 0.5" and 3".

    c.   Edit the letter as follows:

- Replace the word "Student" in the salutation with your name.
- Indent the first line of each paragraph one tab stop.
- Add Mr. Fredlund's title, Circulation Supervisor, on a new line below his name.
- Indent the three-line closing to the second tab stop.

    d.   Spell-check the document.

    e.   Save the letter using the filename FUTURPUB. Print the letter.

4.   You are working on a letter that you will enclose with a scholarship application.

    a.   To see the existing letter, retrieve the file SCHOLAR.

    b.   Set justification to left.

    c.   Set margins to left = 1.25" and right = 1.5".

    d.   Clear all tab settings. Enter new left tabs of 0.5" and 3.25".

    e.   Edit the letter as follows:

- Insert blank lines to begin the letter approximately 2" from the top of the page.
- Using the Date command, enter the current date flush with the right margin as the first line of the letter.
- Indent the first line of each paragraph one tab stop.
- Change the scholarship amount from $2500 to $4200.
- Make the closing begin approximately on position 6.17".
- Indent the closing to the second tab stop.
- Use your name in the closing.

    f.   Using Reveal Codes, delete the current margin setting code.

    g.   Enter new margin settings of left = 1.5" and right = 1.5".

    h.   Spell-check the document.

    i.   Save the letter using the filename APPLICA. Print the letter.

5.   In this problem you will create and format a document.

    a.   Clear the screen for creation of a new document.

    b.   Set justification to ragged right.

    c.   Set margins to left = 2" and right = 1.5".

    d.   Clear all tab settings. Enter new tab settings of .5 and 3" (save with Exit, (F7)).

    e.   Enter the letter below as follows:

- Begin the letter approximately 2.17" from the top of the page.
- Enter the current date using the Date command.
- Display the date flush with the right margin.

- Enter the letter using the approximate line values as a guide.
- Indent each paragraph one tab stop.
- Use your name in the closing.

[current date]

Mr. Jim Class
Public Awareness Coordinator
EAO
893 W. Washington Street
Denver, CO 93823

Dear Mr. Class:

Thank you for taking the time to speak at the Young People's Environmental Awareness meeting yesterday.

We were very pleased with the turnout for your lecture on "How to Save the World in Your Backyard."

I am enclosing the responses to the questionnaire you handed out. I hope you find them helpful for future lectures.

Sincerely,

(your name)

f. Reveal hidden codes.
g. Delete the previous margin setting codes.
h. Enter new margins settings of left = 1.5", right = 1.5".
i. Print the letter.
j. Save the letter using the filename LECTURE.

LAB

Merging and Refining Documents

3

CASE STUDY

Karen Barnes, the membership assistant, submitted the final copy of the welcome letter to the membership coordinator. The membership coordinator is very pleased with the content and form of the welcome letter. However he would like it to be more personalized. He wants to include the first name of the new member and an inside address. Karen will create a form letter using WordPerfect's Merge feature to personalize each welcome letter.

As a second project, he would like Karen to write an article for the club newsletter about the new automatic fee payment program. You will follow Karen as she works on these two projects.

The Merge Feature

Boot the system and if necessary, enter the current date at the DOS date prompt. Load the WordPerfect program.

Retrieve the file WELCOME.

This is the same as the welcome letter you saved as LETTER4 in Lab 2. Notice that the date in the letter is the same as the system date you entered at the DOS prompt. Each time this letter is retrieved or printed, the date will display the system date. This is because of the date code you entered in the document.

Karen needs to change the welcome letter so that each letter sent to a new member is more personal. The welcome letter will include the new member's first name in the salutation and his or her full name and address as the inside address. To do this Karen will use the Merge feature of WordPerfect.

The Merge feature will combine a list of names and addresses that are contained in one file with a form letter in another file. The names and addresses are

OBJECTIVES

In this lab you will learn how to:

1. Use the Merge command.

2. Create primary and the secondary merge files.

3. Merge the primary and secondary files.

4. Center. boldface, and underline text.

5. Open two document files.

6. Create a split screen or open a window.

7. Move text between two documents.

8. Define newspaper-style columns.

9. Reformat the screen display.

10. Use the View Document command.

11. Change justification.

12. Use the Hyphenation feature.

13. Save and exit two document files.

entered (merged) into the form letter in the blank spaces provided. The result is a personalized form letter.

Merge usually requires the use of two files: a **primary file** and a **secondary merge file**. The primary file contains the basic form letter. It directs the merge process through the use of **merge codes**. The merge codes control what information is used from the secondary merge file and where it is entered in the document in the primary file. The welcome letter will be modified to be the primary file.

The secondary merge file, sometimes called an **address file**, contains the information needed to complete the form letter in the primary file. It will contain the new member's name and address data. Each piece of information in the secondary merge file is called a **field**. For example, the member's full name is a field of data, the street address is another field of data, the city a third field of data, and so forth. All the fields of data that are needed to complete the primary document are called a **record**.

The secondary file you will create will contain the following fields of information for each record: Full Name, Street Address, City, State, Zipcode, and First Name. WordPerfect takes the field information from the secondary merge file and combines or merges it into the primary file.

First Karen will modify the welcome letter to accept information from the secondary merge file. Then she will create the secondary merge file, which will hold the new members' names and addresses to be entered into the primary file.

Entering Merge Codes in the Primary File

The welcome letter needs to be modified to allow entry of the name and address information for each new member from the secondary merge file. The inside address will hold the following three lines of information:

> Full Name
> Street Address
> City State Zipcode

The first line of the inside address, which will hold the new member's full name, will be entered as line 5 of the welcome letter.

Move to: Ln 1.67" Pos 1" (blank line above salutation)

How will WordPerfect know to enter the member's full name from the secondary file at this location in the primary file? WordPerfect uses a series of codes, called merge codes, which direct the program to accept information from the secondary merge file at the specified location in the primary file. To display the menu of merge codes use the Tools>Merge Codes or (SHIFT) - (F9) command.

Select: Tools>Merge Codes
   >>   **Merge Codes** (SHIFT) - (F9)

Your display screen should be similar to Figure 3-1.

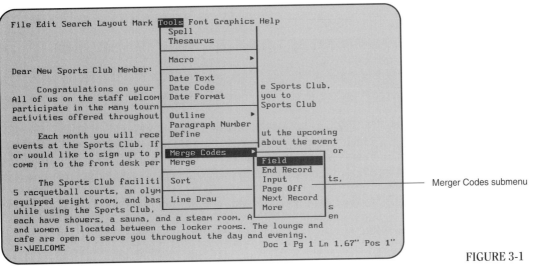

FIGURE 3-1

The Merge Codes submenu (displayed in the status line if you used the function key) consists of five commonly used merge codes. The sixth option, More, allows you to select other merge codes not listed on the menu.

The Merge Codes submenu options have the following meanings:

Field	identifies the field to be inserted from the secondary document into the primary document
End Record	marks the end of a record in the secondary file
Input	stops the merge and waits for keyboard input
Page Off	instructs WordPerfect not to place page breaks after each primary file
Next Record	instructs WordPerfect to move to the next secondary file record during the merge

A Field merge code needs to be entered in the primary file for each field of data you want copied from the secondary file. The location of the Field merge code directs WordPerfect where to enter the data. The cursor is positioned on the line where the new member's full name will appear as the first line of the inside address. The first field you will identify, then, is the Full Name field.

Select: Field

The prompt "Enter field:" is displayed in the status line. Following the prompt you must enter the name you want to assign to the first Field merge code. A field name should be short and descriptive of the contents of the field. You will use the field name "Name."

Type: Name
Press: ⏎

Your display screen should be similar to Figure 3-2.

FIGURE 3-2

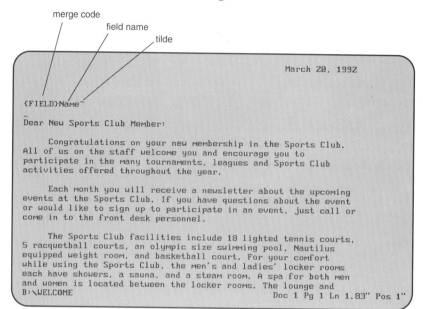

The Field merge code, {FIELD}, followed by the name you assigned the field is displayed at the cursor location. The ~ (tilde) at the end of the field name tells WordPerfect where the field name ends. When the command to merge the documents is used, the information for the new member's full name from the secondary merge file will be entered at this location in the primary file.

The next line of the inside address will contain the street address. To create and move to the next line,

Press: ⏎

To enter the Field merge code for the street address,

Select: Tools>Merge Codes>Field
>> Merge Codes (SHIFT) - (F9), Field

This time, in response to the field name prompt,

Type: Address
Press: ⏎

The second Field merge code is displayed in the welcome letter.

The next line of the inside address will display three fields of data from the secondary file: city, state, and zipcode. They will be identified by the field names City, State, and Zip.

Press: ⏎

To enter the merge code for the next field of data,

Select: Tools>Merge Codes>Field
  >>   Merge Codes (SHIFT) - (F9), Field

Type: City
Press: ⏎

To separate the City field from the next field,

Press: Space bar

The State field will be entered on the same line as the City field.

Select: Tools>Merge Codes>Field
  >>   Merge Codes (SHIFT) - (F9), Field
Type: State
Press: ⏎

To separate the State field from the next field, Zipcode, and enter the field name,

Press: Space bar (2 times)
Select: Tools>Merge Codes>Field
      >> Merge Codes (SHIFT) - (F9), Field
Type: Zip
Press: ⏎

To enter a blank line between the inside address and the salutation,

Press: ⏎

Your display screen should be similar to Figure 3-3.

FIGURE 3-3

```
                                                   March 20, 1992


{FIELD}Name~
{FIELD}Address~
{FIELD}City~, {FIELD}State~ {FIELD}Zip~
_
Dear New Sports Club Member:

        Congratulations on your new membership in the Sports Club.
All of us on the staff welcome you and encourage you to
participate in the many tournaments, leagues and Sports Club
activities offered throughout the year.

        Each month you will receive a newsletter about the upcoming
events at the Sports Club. If you have questions about the event
or would like to sign up to participate in an event, just call or
come in to the front desk personnel.

        The Sports Club facilities include 18 lighted tennis courts,
5 racquetball courts, an olympic size swimming pool, Nautilus
equipped weight room, and basketball court. For your comfort
while using the Sports Club, the men's and ladies' locker rooms
B:\WELCOME                              Doc 1 Pg 1 Ln 2.17" Pos 1"
```

The merge codes to enter the inside address data from the secondary merge file are now complete. If you have made an error, you can edit the merge codes just like any other text entry.

The last field of information (field 6) that needs to be entered in the primary file is the new member's first name in the salutation. First the words "New Sports Club Member" need to be deleted.

Move to: Ln 2.33" Pos 1.5" ("N" of "New")
Press: (CTRL) - (END)

To enter the merge code for the first name (field 6) into the salutation,

Select: Tools>Merge Codes>Field
>> Merge Codes (SHIFT) - (F9), Field
Type: FirstName
Press: (⏎)

To end the salutation with a colon,

Type: :

Once all the merge codes that are needed in the primary file are correctly entered, the file must be saved.

A few notes about entering field merge codes in the primary document before saving the file:

■ A field name can be used more than one time in the primary document. For example, the Name field could be used again in the letter without assigning it a new field name.

- The field name should be short and descriptive. It can be a single word or multiple words. If you enter multiple words use a hyphen or underscore to separate the words. Do not use a blank space between words.

- Not all the fields in the secondary file need to be used in the primary file.

To save the primary file as **WELCOME.PF** (the extension .PF identifies the file as a primary file) and clear the screen in preparation for creating the secondary merge file,

Select:	File>Exit
>>	**Exit** (F7)
Type:	**Y**
Type:	**WELCOME.PF**
Press:	(↵)
Type:	**N**

Creating the Secondary File

A blank Wordperfect screen is ready to be used to enter the fields and records for the secondary merge file. The secondary merge file will hold the six fields of data about each new member. The six fields of data for each new member form a record of information.

The primary file calls for the following six fields of data for each record:

Field Number	Field Name
Field 1	Name
Field 2	Address
Field 3	City
Field 4	State
Field 5	Zip
Field 6	FirstName

When entering the data for the secondary merge file, the following rules must be observed:

- At the beginning of the document enter a merge code which identifies the names of each field used in the primary file.

- The order of fields in the primary file determines what order the fields of data should be listed in the secondary merge file. For example, the FirstName field in the primary file is the sixth field of data in a record from the secondary merge file.

- The end of a field of data is marked with an End Field merge code.

- The end of a record is marked with an End Record merge code.

- Each field of data must be entered in the same sequence for all records and must contain the same type of information.

- The same number of fields must appear in each record.

WORD PROCESSING

To enter the merge code that identifies the field names,

Select: Tools>Merge Codes>More
>> Merge Codes (SHIFT) - (F9), More

Your display screen should be similar to Figure 3-4.

FIGURE 3-4

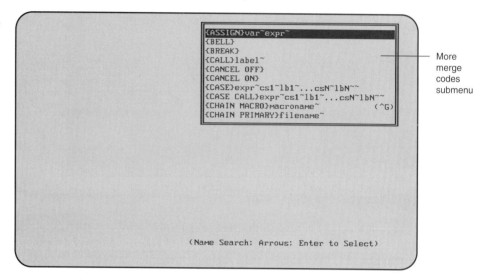

A submenu of other merge codes is displayed. They are listed in alphabetical order. You can use the ⊤ and ⊥ keys to move the highlight bar through the list of codes, or you can use the mouse. If you use the mouse, position the mouse pointer inside the Merge Codes selection box and drag the mouse to move the highlight. The list will scroll as you drag the mouse. You can also move by "pages" using the (PGDN) or (PGUP) keys.

Using any of these methods, move the highlight to {FIELD NAMES}. To select it,

Press: (↵) (or press the right mouse button)

The prompt "Enter Field 1:" appears in the status line. In response to the prompt you need to enter the field name of the first field. The field name must be entered exactly as you typed it in the primary file.

Type: Name
Press: (↵)

WordPerfect displays a prompt asking you to enter the name of the second field.

Type: Address
Press: (↵)

Continue to define the remaining four field names (City, State, Zip, and FirstName). When WordPerfect prompts you to enter the field name for the seventh field,

Press: (↵)

This tells WordPerfect that you are finished. When you are done your screen should be similar to Figure 3-5.

FIGURE 3-5

The {FIELD NAMES} definition code is displayed on the first line of the screen. The name of each field as you typed it and a tilde at the end of each field name are included. The code ends with an extra tilde and an {END RECORD} merge code. WordPerfect treats this merge code as a special record in the secondary file. The page break line separates this record from the other records you will be entering into the document next.

The first record begins immediately below the special record. Your cursor should be on the first line of page 2. Notice that the status line displays "Field: Name." This tells you WordPerfect is ready for you to enter the first field of data, the new member's full name.

Type: **Mr. Anthony R. Myers** (do not press (⏎))

To tell the program that this is the end of the first field of data, you must enter the End Field merge code. This code can be entered easily using the (F9) key, or it can be entered using Tools>Merge Codes> More>{End Field}. Since pressing (F9) is much easier, to enter this code,

Press: End Field (F9)

The End Field code is entered after the first field, and the cursor moves down one line. WordPerfect displays "Field: Address" in the status line to tell you it expects you to enter the data for this field next.

Type: **1452 Southern Ave.**
Press: End Field (F9)

Enter the information for the remaining fields as follows:

Type: **Mesa**
Press: End Field (F9)

Type:	AZ
Press:	End Field (F9)

Type:	85202
Press:	End Field (F9)

Type:	Anthony
Press:	End Field (F9)

The six fields of information, corresponding to the six field merge codes used in the inside address and saluatation in the primary file, are complete for the first record in the secondary merge file.

To separate this record from the next record and to indicate a page break between documents, the End Record merge code is entered. To enter this code,

Select:	Tools>Merge Codes>End Record
>>	Merge Codes (SHIFT) - (F9), End Record

Your display screen should be similar to Figure 3-6.

FIGURE 3-6

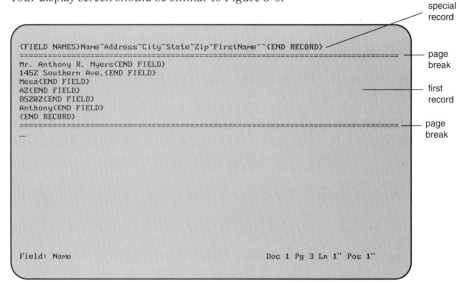

An {END RECORD} code is entered on the line, and the cursor moves to the next line in the file. A double dashed line separates each record. This line indicates a page break. It tells WordPerfect to begin a new page following the page break.

Never separate fields or records with an extra hard carriage return. Also do not insert spaces following the last word in a field and a End Record merge code.

Enter the field information for the second record as follows:

Type:	Miss Allycin Miller
Press:	End Field (F9)

Type:	128 Forest Ave.
Press:	End Field (F9)

Type:	Tempe
Press:	End Field (F9)

Type:	AZ
Press:	End Field (F9)

Type:	85285
Press:	End Field (F9)

Type:	Allycin
Press:	End Field (F9)

Select:	Tools>Merge Codes>End Record
>>	Merge Codes (SHIFT) - (F9), End Record

Your display screen should be similar to Figure 3-7.

FIGURE 3-7

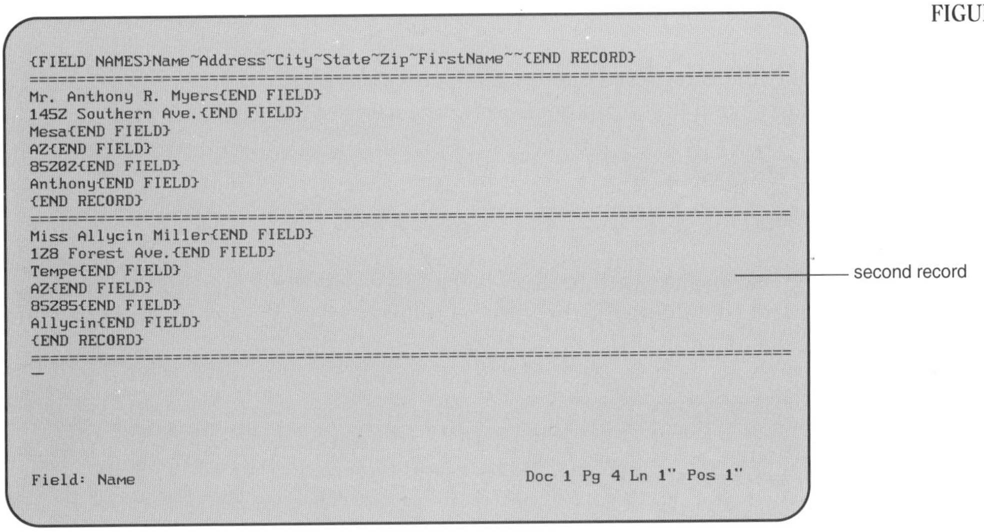

```
{FIELD NAMES}Name~Address~City~State~Zip~FirstName~~{END RECORD}
=================================================================
Mr. Anthony R. Myers{END FIELD}
1452 Southern Ave.{END FIELD}
Mesa{END FIELD}
AZ{END FIELD}
85202{END FIELD}
Anthony{END FIELD}
{END RECORD}
=================================================================
Miss Allycin Miller{END FIELD}
128 Forest Ave.{END FIELD}
Tempe{END FIELD}                                    ——— second record
AZ{END FIELD}
85285{END FIELD}
Allycin{END FIELD}
{END RECORD}
=================================================================
_

Field: Name                          Doc 1 Pg 4 Ln 1" Pos 1"
```

Enter your name and address as the third record in the secondary file.
Check your screen and make any corrections as needed. Make sure each field ends with an End Field code and that each record ends with an End Record code.

The number of records you enter into the secondary file is limited only by your diskette space.

To save the secondary file using the file name WELCOME.SF (the file extension .SF identifies this file as the secondary file) and clear the screen in preparation for merging the primary file with the secondary merge file,

Select:	File>Exit
>>	Exit (F7)
Press:	Y
Type:	WELCOME.SF
Press:	(⏎)
Type:	N

A blank WordPerfect screen is ready for use.

Merging the Primary and Secondary Merge Files

Now that you have created and saved the primary and secondary merge files, you are ready to combine them to create the new personalized welcome letter.

During this process a third file is created. The original primary and secondary files are not altered or affected in any way. The third file is the result of the merging of the primary and secondary files. It is very important to clear the screen of any document before merging files.

Select: Tools>Merge
   >>   Merge (CTRL) - (F9), Merge

In response to the prompt to enter the name of the primary file,

Type: WELCOME.PF
Press: (⏎)

The primary file is retrieved into the computer's memory.

Next respond to the prompt to enter the name of the secondary file:

Type: WELCOME.SF
Press: (⏎)

The status line displays the message "* Merging *." At the completion of the merge, the document containing the three letters is displayed on the screen. To move to the top of the document,

Press: (HOME) (HOME) (↑)

Your display screen should be similar to Figure 3-8.

FIGURE 3-8

```
                                                    March 20, 1992


Mr. Anthony R. Myers
1452 Southern Ave.
Mesa, AZ 85202

Dear Anthony:

     Congratulations on your new membership in the Sports Club.
All of us on the staff welcome you and encourage you to
participate in the many tournaments, leagues and Sports Club
activities offered throughout the year.

     Each month you will receive a newsletter about the upcoming
events at the Sports Club. If you have questions about the event
or would like to sign up to participate in an event, just call or
come in to the front desk personnel.

     The Sports Club facilities include 18 lighted tennis courts,
5 racquetball courts, an olympic size swimming pool, Nautilus
equipped weight room, and basketball court. For your comfort
while using the Sports Club, the men's and ladies' locker rooms
                                           Doc 1 Pg 1 Ln 1" Pos 1"
```

The personalized letter to Anthony Myers is displayed. The fields of data from the secondary merge file have been entered into the primary file at the location of the merge codes.

To see the letter using the data for the second record,

Press: (PGDN)

Finally, to see the letter containing your name and address information,

Press: (PGDN)

Now each time Karen needs to send welcome letters, all she needs to do is to create the new member secondary merge file and issue the Merge command. Because the Date command was used, the date will automatically reflect the date the letter was created.

Save (F10) the current document of three welcome letters as WELCOME.MRG. The letters can be printed like any other document. Print the letter containing your name and address information only. Remember to select the appropriate printer for your microcomputer system first.

To leave the document and clear the screen,

Select: File>Exit
    >>   Exit (F7)
Type: N
Type: N

To review, the steps in creating a customized form letter are:

1.   Create the primary file. Enter Field merge codes in the document to tell WordPerfect where and what fields of information to use from the secondary merge file. Save the document as the primary file.

2.   Create the secondary merge file. It will contain the special record which identifies the field names used in the primary file and the variable data or information needed to complete the primary file for each record. Each field of data must end with an End Field code. Each record must end with an End Record code. As many records as diskette space will allow can be entered in this file.

3.   Use the Merge command to combine the primary and secondary files to create a customized document for each record in the secondary merge file.

Centering and Boldfacing Text

The second project Karen needs to work on is the article for the newsletter about the new automatic fee payment program. The membership coordinator already has a file started which contains another article to be entered in the newsletter. He has asked Karen to enter her article at the end of this document.

Retrieve the file ARTICLE.DOC.

Your display screen should be similar to Figure 3-9.

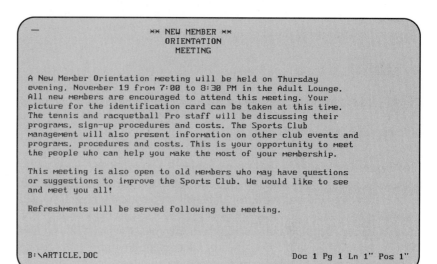

```
 —                      ** NEW MEMBER **
                           ORIENTATION
                             MEETING

A New Member Orientation meeting will be held on Thursday
evening, November 19 from 7:00 to 8:30 PM in the Adult Lounge.
All new members are encouraged to attend this meeting. Your
picture for the identification card can be taken at this time.
The tennis and racquetball Pro staff will be discussing their
programs, sign-up procedures and costs. The Sports Club
management will also present information on other club events and
programs, procedures and costs. This is your opportunity to meet
the people who can help you make the most of your membership.

This meeting is also open to old members who may have questions
or suggestions to improve the Sports Club. We would like to see
and meet you all!

Refreshments will be served following the meeting.



B:\ARTICLE.DOC                              Doc 1 Pg 1 Ln 1" Pos 1"
```

FIGURE 3-9

An article concerning a new member orientation meeting is displayed on the screen.

Karen will begin the article about the automatic fee payment program three lines below the end of the first article. To move to this location,

Press: (HOME) (HOME) (↓)

The cursor should be on Ln 4.67" Pos 1" (three blank lines below the last line of text).

She would like to enter a title for her article similar to the title in the article on the display screen. Notice that each line of this title is centered between the margins. If you have a color monitor, you will also note that it is displayed in color. This is because it has been formatted to be printed in boldface print.

The title for her article is: NEW PROGRAM AUTOMATIC PAYMENT. She will enter it on three lines.

To turn on the capability to enter text in all capital letters,

Press: (CAPS LOCK)

Notice in the status line that "POS" is displayed in uppercase letters. This is how WordPerfect tells you that the (CAPS LOCK) key is on. The (CAPS LOCK) key affects only alphabet keys. Other characters will require that you use the (SHIFT) key.

To **center** text between the margins, the Center (Layout>Align>Center or (SHIFT)-(F6)) command is used. The cursor must be positioned on the left margin before using the command. Otherwise the text will be centered between the cursor location and the right margin.

Select: Layout>Align>Center
>> Center (SHIFT) - (F6)

The cursor jumps to the middle of the screen. As text is typed, it will be centered between the current margin settings.

Karen also wants the title to be printed in **boldface** characters. Boldface text is printed darker than normal text. On the screen it is displayed brighter than surrounding text or in color if you have a color monitor. The command to produce boldfaced text is Bold, (Font>Appearance>Bold or (F6)). To mark the area in the document to begin bold text and enter the first line of the title,

Select: Font>Appearance>Bold
>> Bold (F6)
Type: ** NEW PROGRAM **
Press: (↵)

The text is displayed brighter on your screen or in color if you have a color monitor, to show the area that is to be printed in bold text. If yours is not brighter, you may need to adjust the contrast and brightness of your monitor.

Before entering the second line of the heading, the Center command must be used again. Each line you want centered must begin with the Center command. The Bold command continues in effect until turned off by selecting the command again. Since it is quicker to use the function key to initiate the Center command, to center this line,

Press: Center (SHIFT) - (F6)
Type: AUTOMATIC
Press: (↵)
Press: Center (SHIFT) - (F6)
Type: PAYMENT

To end boldfacing using the function key command and turn off all capital letters,

Press: Bold (F6)
Press: (CAPS LOCK)

Karen will begin the text of the article two lines below the heading. To create the blank lines and move to this location,

Press: (↵) (3 times)

Your cursor should now be on Ln 5.5" Pos 1". Your display screen should be similar to Figure 3-10.

FIGURE 3-10

```
A New Member Orientation meeting will be held on Thursday
evening, November 19 from 7:00 to 8:30 PM in the Adult Lounge.
All new members are encouraged to attend this meeting. Your
picture for the identification card can be taken at this time.
The tennis and racquetball Pro staff will be discussing their
programs, sign-up procedures and costs. The Sports Club
management will also present information on other club events and
programs, procedures and costs. This is your opportunity to meet
the people who can help you make the most of your membership.

This meeting is also open to old members who may have questions
or suggestions to improve the Sports Club. We would like to see
and meet you all!

Refreshments will be served following the meeting.


                    ** NEW PROGRAM **
                        AUTOMATIC
                        PAYMENT



B:\ARTICLE.DOC                              Doc 1 Pg 1 Ln 5.5" Pos 1"
```

Using Two Document Files

Now Karen could begin typing the information about the automatic fee payment program into the document. However, she doesn't want to retype the same information that is in the welcome letter. Instead she will copy the paragraph about the automatic fee payment program from the WELCOME file into the document on the display.

To do this she will use the WordPerfect Switch feature. This feature will let her use two document files at the same time. It does this by creating a new screen for the second document file.

To create a new screen and switch to that screen, the Switch (Edit>Switch Document or (SHIFT) - (F3)) command is used.

Select: **E**dit>**S**witch Document

>> Switch (SHIFT) - (F3)

The screen is blank. The status line indicates, however, that you are in document 2. The ARTICLE.DOC file is still in the computer's memory as document 1, although it is not displayed.

At this point new text could be entered to create a new document, or an existing document can be retrieved. Karen will retrieve the WELCOME file into the new screen.

Retrieve WELCOME.

The welcome letter is displayed on the screen as document 2. Two files are now open and can be used at the same time.

To see and use the file ARTICLE.DOC in the document 1 screen, use Edit>Switch Document or Switch (SHIFT) - (F3) again. It now acts as a toggle to move between the two document screens. Since the function key is quicker,

Press: (SHIFT) - (F3)

The file ARTICLE.DOC is displayed in the document 1 screen.

The two files can be seen and used by switching from one document screen to another using (SHIFT)-(F3) or Edit>Switch Document.

Creating a Split Screen

It would be even more convenient for Karen if she could see both documents at the same time on the display screen. This can be done by splitting the display screen into two parts, or **windows**, using the Screen (Edit>Window or (CTRL) - (F3)) command.

Select: **E**dit>**W**indow
      >>   Screen (CTRL) - (F3), **W**indow

The prompt "Number of lines in this window: 24" is displayed in the status line. This is the default window-size setting for a full screen of 24 lines. To divide the full screen into two equal halves,

Type: **12**

Press: (⏎)

Your display screen should be similar to Figure 3-11.

FIGURE 3-11

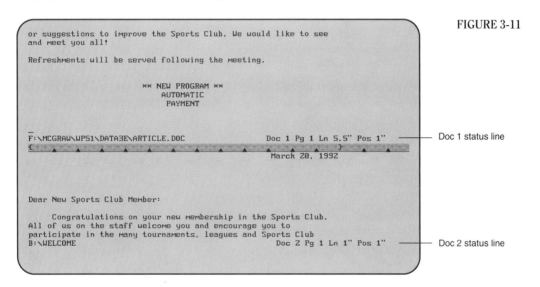

Doc 1 status line

Doc 2 status line

The screen is divided into two equal parts by a reverse-video bar marked by triangles, which represent the tab stops. Document 1 is displayed in the top window. Document 2 is displayed in the bottom window. The status line at the bottom of each window identifies the file and cursor location.

The cursor is currently located in document 1. You could now edit the file in this window without affecting the file in document 2. To switch into document 2,

Press: Switch (SHIFT) - (F3)

The cursor has jumped into document 2.

Note: Mouse users can click on the window to switch from one document to another.

Now you could edit the document in this window without affecting the file in the other window. Notice as you switch from one window to the other that the triangles within the reverse video bar change direction. They point upward when the cursor is in the upper window and downward when the cursor is in the lower window.

The cursor movement keys and command keys operate as they would if only one window or one file was open.

Moving Text Between Documents

Now Karen is ready to move a copy of the paragraph on the automatic fee payment program from the WELCOME file (document 2) into the ARTICLE.DOC file (document 1).

The paragraph to be copied is the fifth paragraph. Using the ⊕ key and the status line in document 2 to locate your cursor position,

Move to: Ln 6.17" Pos 1" (left margin of first line of fifth paragraph)

Next, to issue the Move command,

Select: **E**dit>**S**elect>**P**aragraph
   >>   Move (CTRL) - (F4), **P**aragraph

The whole paragraph is highlighted. The menu displayed in the Status line lets you select whether you want to cut, copy, or delete the marked (highlighted) section of text. To copy the block,

Select: **C**opy

A copy of the paragraph is stored in temporary memory. Karen wants to insert the copy of the paragraph into the ARTICLE.DOC file in document 1. To do this you will switch into document 1 and then retrieve the paragraph from temporary memory.

Press: Switch (SHIFT) - (F3)

The cursor jumps back into document 1. It should be three lines below the heading (Ln 5.5" Pos 1"). If it is not there, before continuing, move it to that location.

To retrieve the paragraph into document 1,

Press: (⏎)

The paragraph is copied into the file in document 1. To see the rest of the paragraph,

Move to: Ln 6.67" Pos 1" (last line of paragraph)

Your display screen should be similar to Figure 3-12.

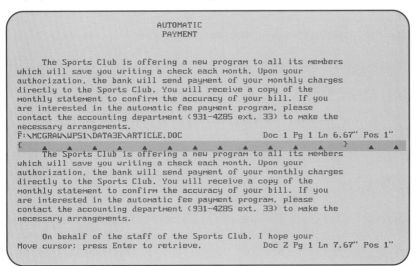

```
                           AUTOMATIC
                           PAYMENT

        The Sports Club is offering a new program to all its members
   which will save you writing a check each month. Upon your
   authorization, the bank will send payment of your monthly charges
   directly to the Sports Club. You will receive a copy of the
   monthly statement to confirm the accuracy of your bill. If you
   are interested in the automatic fee payment program, please
   contact the accounting department (931-4285 ext. 33) to make the
   necessary arrangements.
   F:\MCGRAW\WP51\DATA3E\ARTICLE.DOC          Doc 1 Pg 1 Ln 6.67" Pos 1"
   {    ▲     ▲       ▲      ▲      ▲      ▲      ▲     ▲    }    ▲      ▲
        The Sports Club is offering a new program to all its members
   which will save you writing a check each month. Upon your
   authorization, the bank will send payment of your monthly charges
   directly to the Sports Club. You will receive a copy of the
   monthly statement to confirm the accuracy of your bill. If you
   are interested in the automatic fee payment program, please
   contact the accounting department (931-4285 ext. 33) to make the
   necessary arrangements.

        On behalf of the staff of the Sports Club, I hope your
   Move cursor; press Enter to retrieve.       Doc 2 Pg 1 Ln 7.67" Pos 1"
```

FIGURE 3-12

The copy of the paragraph has been copied from the file in document 2 and inserted into the file in document 1. Using the Split Screen feature to view both documents at the same time made this process very easy.

The documents in each window operate independently of each other. The changes that are made in one document do not affect the other. You can also use the split screen to view two different parts of the same document at the same time.

Closing a Split Screen

Karen no longer needs to see the WELCOME file in document 2. To return to displaying a single document on the screen at one time, the process of creating a window is reversed.

Select: Edit>Window
   >>   Screen (CTRL) - (F3), Window

To return to a full screen of 24 lines,

Type: 24
Press: ⏎

Your display screen should be similar to Figure 3-13.

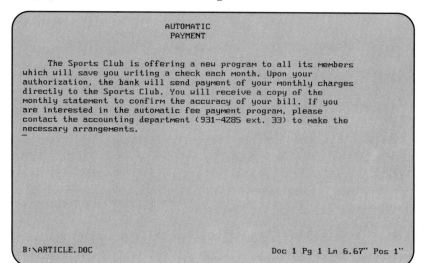

```
                         AUTOMATIC
                          PAYMENT


        The Sports Club is offering a new program to all its members
    which will save you writing a check each month. Upon your
    authorization, the bank will send payment of your monthly charges
    directly to the Sports Club. You will receive a copy of the
    monthly statement to confirm the accuracy of your bill. If you
    are interested in the automatic fee payment program, please
    contact the accounting department (931-4285 ext. 33) to make the
    necessary arrangements.




    B:\ARTICLE.DOC                               Doc 1 Pg 1 Ln 6.67" Pos 1"
```

FIGURE 3-13

The screen display returns to a single window of 24 lines, and document 1 occupies the whole screen. Both documents, however, are still open. But document 2 is not visible on the display. When closing a window, the document the cursor is positioned in is the document that will be displayed.

To continue her work on the article, Karen wants to remove the indentation from the first line in the paragraph. To do this she could use the Reveal Codes screen to locate the position of the tab code and then delete it. However, she is sure the tab code is located at the beginning of the line that is indented. So she will remove the code while in normal document display.

Move to: Ln 5.5" Pos 1" (left margin of first line)
Press: (DEL)

The tab code has been deleted, and the line is no longer indented.

Underlining Text

Finally, Karen wants to **underline** the accounting department telephone number. To underline text which is already entered in a document, the area of text to be underlined must first be defined using the Block feature.

To position the cursor under the "9" in the telephone number, and to turn Block on,

Move to: Ln 6.5" Pos 4.5" ("9" in telephone number)
Select: Edit>Block
    >>   Block (ALT)-(F4)

To define the block of text to be underlined (the entire telephone number),

Move to: Ln 6.5" Pos 6.1" (the "3" at end of telephone number)

The telephone number is highlighted on the screen.

To mark this block of text to be underlined, the Underline (Font>Appearance>Underline or (F8)) command is used.

Select: Font>Appearance>Underline
>>   Underline (F8)

Your display screen should be similar to Figure 3-14.

FIGURE 3-14

```
                        AUTOMATIC
                        PAYMENT


        The Sports Club is offering a new program to all its members
    which will save you writing a check each month. Upon your
    authorization, the bank will send payment of your monthly charges
    directly to the Sports Club. You will receive a copy of the
    monthly statement to confirm the accuracy of your bill. If you
    are interested in the automatic fee payment program, please
    contact the accounting department (931-4285 ext. 33) to make the
    necessary arrangements.




    B:\ARTICLE.DOC                          Doc 1 Pg 1 Ln 6.5" Pos 6.1"
```

The marked block of text is underlined, highlighted, or displayed in color, depending upon your monitor. When it is printed, it will be underlined. The hidden code to turn underlining on and off is placed at the beginning and end of the block.

If you want to underline text as you enter it into the document, simply select Underline before typing the text. It then must be turned off by selecting Underline again at the end of the text to be underlined. It is much quicker to use the function key, (F8), to initiate this command than it is to use the pull-down menus.

Defining Columns

The articles will appear in the newsletter as long newspaper-style columns. The WordPerfect Columns (Layout>Columns or (ALT) - (F7)) command lets you easily set the text format of a document into columns.

As with many WordPerfect commands, a hidden code is entered into the document to control the display of the text. The location of the hidden code indicates the point in the document at which the command will take effect. Since both articles need to be displayed in a column format, move the cursor to the top of page 1.

Press: (PGUP)
Select: Layout>Columns
>>   Columns/Table (ALT) - (F7), **C**olumns

The Columns submenu (displayed in the status line if you used the function key command) lists three options: On, Off, and Define. They have the following effect:

On   turns columns on at the cursor position
Off   turns columns off at the cursor position
Define defines the type, spacing, and number of columns

To use the Columns feature, you must first define the column settings.

Select: Define

Your display screen should be similar to Figure 3-15.

FIGURE 3-15

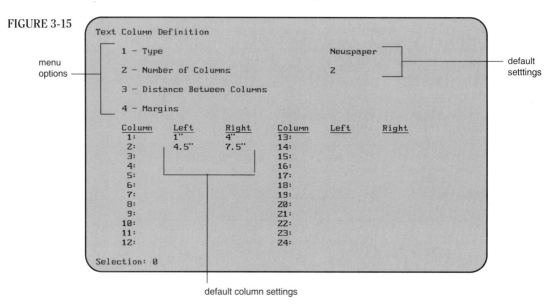

default column settings

The Text Column Definition menu replaces the document on the screen. Four menu options are displayed in the upper portion of the screen. The default settings are displayed in the column to the right of each option. The lower portion of the screen shows the right and left margins for the columns based upon the default settings.

The first menu option, Type, lets you specify the type of column you want to create.

Select: Type

The three types of columns which can be created are displayed in the menu in the status line: 1 Newspaper, 2 Parallel, and 3 Parallel with Block Protect. With **newspaper columns**, text runs vertically up and down the page through the columns. With **parallel columns**, text runs horizontally across the page. One of the columns may spill over to the next page while the other does not. The third type of column, Parallel with Block protect, is the same as parallel columns, except that text is protected from being split between two pages.

The default setting is Newspaper. Since the default setting is acceptable, this option does not need to be changed. To leave this menu without changing the default,

Press: ⏎

The second option, 2 Number of Columns, lets you specify how many columns of text you want across the width of the page. The Sports Club newsletter has three columns.

Select: Number of Columns

The cursor is positioned under the default setting. To change the number of columns to three,

Type: 3
Press: ⏎

Your display screen should be similar to Figure 3-16.

FIGURE 3-16

```
Text Column Definition

    1 - Type                        Newspaper

    2 - Number of Columns           3

    3 - Distance Between Columns

    4 - Margins

    Column   Left     Right     Column   Left     Right
      1:     1"       2.83"       13:
      2:     3.33"    5.17"       14:
      3:     5.67"    7.5"        15:
      4:                          16:
      5:                          17:
      6:                          18:
      7:                          19:
      8:                          20:
      9:                          21:
     10:                          22:
     11:                          23:
     12:                          24:

Selection: 0
```

new column settings

Wordperfect automatically calculates and displays the new left and right margins for the three columns in the lower portion of the screen. The first column will begin at the left default margin of 1" and end at 2.83". The second column will begin at 3.33" and end at 5.16" . The third column will begin at 5.67" and end at the right default margin setting of 7.5".

The next option, 3 Distance Between Columns, lets you specify how much space you want between the columns.

Select: Distance Between Columns

The default setting of .5" is displayed. Karen thinks the default setting will be suitable, and decides to leave it as it is.

Press: ⏎

You can also change the default left and right margins by selecting the Margins option. However, for our purposes, the default settings are acceptable. To save the column definitions and exit the menu,

Press: F7 or ⏎

The column settings have been defined. A hidden code, [Col Def], containing the column definitions has been entered into the document.

The Columns menu is displayed in the status line again. It allows you to continue making selections. Next you need to direct the program to display the document using the column settings defined. This will enter a [Col on] code in the document. To turn the display of columns on,

Select: On

Reformatting the Screen Display

It appears that nothing has happened. To reformat the display of the text to the new column settings, you could move down through the document using (PGDN) or the cursor movement keys. However, a faster way is to use the Rewrite command, an option in the Screen menu.

Press: Screen (CTRL) - (F3)
Select: Rewrite

The text is reformatted so that it is in newspaper-style columns. Your display screen should be similar to Figure 3-17.

FIGURE 3-17

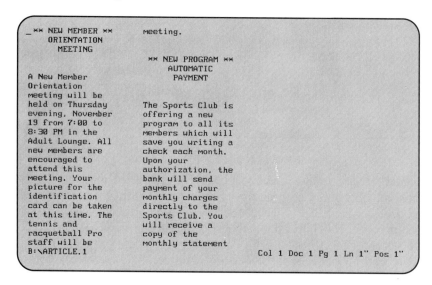

```
_ ** NEW MEMBER **        meeting.
     ORIENTATION
     MEETING
                              ** NEW PROGRAM **
                                  AUTOMATIC
A New Member                       PAYMENT
Orientation
meeting will be
held on Thursday
evening, November      The Sports Club is
19 from 7:00 to        offering a new
8:30 PM in the         program to all its
Adult Lounge. All      members which will
new members are        save you writing a
encouraged to          check each month.
attend this            Upon your
meeting. Your          authorization, the
picture for the        bank will send
identification         payment of your
card can be taken      monthly charges
at this time. The      directly to the
tennis and             Sports Club. You
racquetball Pro        will receive a
staff will be          copy of the
B:\ARTICLE.1           monthly statement      Col 1 Doc 1 Pg 1 Ln 1" Pos 1"
```

The two articles appear on the screen as two columns of text. Using this option quickly reformats the screen display to the new settings.

To move to the bottom of the page,

Press: (CTRL) - (HOME) (↓)

The cursor is positioned on the last line of the second column. The second column ends before the last line of the page. If there were more text in the second column, it would wrap to the top of the third column.

The following keys can be used to move around the document while in column format:

Key	Action
⟨↑⟩, ⟨↓⟩, or ⟨PGDN⟩	scroll all columns at the same time
⟨→⟩, ⟨←⟩, or ⟨HOME⟩	move cursor inside a column
⟨CTRL⟩ - ⟨HOME⟩ ⟨→⟩	move cursor from one column to another
⟨CTRL⟩ - ⟨HOME⟩ ⟨←⟩	
⟨PGUP⟩	move cursor to top of first column

Try moving the cursor around the columns. When you are done, use ⟨PGUP⟩ to return to the top of the first column.

To edit text while in column format, the delete keys all work within a single column. As in regular document display, the text is automatically reformatted on a line when insertions and deletions are made. You can use most WordPerfect features when in column format, with the exception of Column Definition, Document Comments, Footnotes, and Margins.

In some cases it may be easier to turn off the display of columns, do the editing and changes to the text that are needed, and then turn the column display back on. The display of columns is turned off by selecting the Columns Off/On option in the Columns menu. A [Col off] code is hidden in the document to control the display.

Note: Be careful when turning columns on or off. If the command is not entered in the proper location in the document, any text located between the on and off codes is formatted in columns. The original column definition settings remain in effect in the document unless the code is deleted or another column definition is entered.

Viewing the Document

Before Karen prints the article she wants to view it on the screen as it will appear when printed. The View Document option in the Print menu lets you see how different formats and settings will appear when the document is printed.

To see how the columns will appear when printed,

Select: **F**ile>**P**rint>**V**iew Document
  >>   Print ⟨SHIFT⟩ - ⟨F7⟩, **V**iew Document

After a few moments, the text is generated and displayed in the view document screen. Your display screen should be similar to Figure 3-18 on the next page.

The full page is displayed as close in appearance as possible to the printed page. WordPerfect can display the entire page by changing to a graphics display mode rather than the text display mode.

Note: If your computer does not have graphics capabilities, the View Document feature displays the document in text mode. The instructions in the rest of this

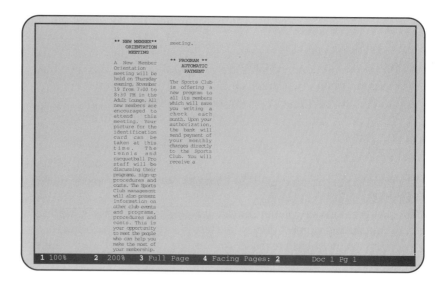

FIGURE 3-18

section do not apply to your computer system. Instead, to see the lower half of the document press (CTRL) (HOME) (↓). To leave the View screen press (F7). Continue the lab by skipping to the next section, "Changing Justification."

The menu at the bottom of the screen lets you enlarge the viewed document. To view the document at its actual size (100%),

Press: 1

Your display screen should be similar to Figure 3-19.

FIGURE 3-19

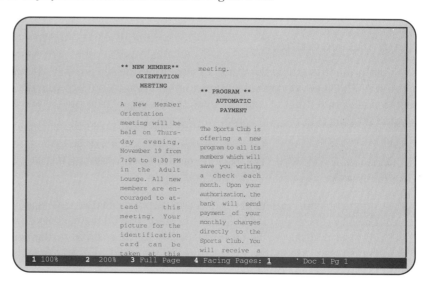

Now the text is large enough to read easily. Because most monitors are not large enough to display an entire page at full size, only the upper postion of the article is visible. To move to the bottom of the page,

Press: (CTRL) - (HOME) (↓)

Karen is not pleased with how the articles will appear when printed. She does not like the large gaps which appear between words. The gaps occur because the justification setting is Full, forcing the program to insert spaces between words to make the right and left margins even. She also does not like how the last line of the first article appears at the top of the second column.

To leave the View screen,

Press: **Exit** (F7)

Changing Justification

Karen would like to see how the document will appear if the justification setting is changed to Left. To make this change,

Press: (PGUP)
Select: **Layout>Line>Justification>Left**
   >>   Format (SHIFT) - (F8), **Line>** Justification>Left
Press: Exit (F7)

The change in the justification setting does not affect the screen display since the text is displayed with left justification only. When printed, the right margins will be printed as they appear on the screen.

If your computer has graphics capabilities, view the change in the document by selecting **F**ile>**P**rint>**V**iew Document or Print (SHIFT)-(F7), **V**iew Document. You will see that the right margins are no longer even and the large gaps between words have been eliminated. However, now the large gap appears at the right margin, making the right margin too ragged. To leave the View screen, press Exit (F7).

On lines of text where there are several short words, the wrapping of text to the next line is not a problem. On lines where there are long words, the long word is wrapped to the next line, leaving a large gap on the previous line. Hyphenating a long word at the end of a line will help solve this problem.

Using Hyphenation

WordPerfect's Hyphenation feature fits as much of a word as possible on a line before hyphenating the word. The balance of the word wraps to the next line. Hyphenation is set to off by default. To turn it on,

Select: **Layout>Line> Hyphenation>Yes**
   >>   Format (SHIFT) - (F8), **Line>**Hyphenation>Yes

To leave the Line Format menu,

Press: **Exit** (F7)

To reformat the screen display,

Press: Screen (CTRL) - (F3), **R**ewrite

Your screen should be similar to Figure 3-20.

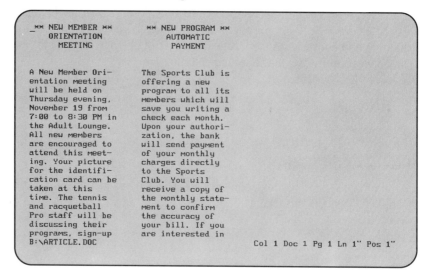

FIGURE 3-20

WordPerfect adds hyphenation to the document. The hyphenation points are determined automatically, based upon the U.S spelling dictionary rules. This dictionary is included in the WordPerfect 5.1 program. If WordPerfect cannot determine how to hyphenate a word, it will prompt you to position the hyphen in any long word that needs hyphenation. The prompt "Position hyphen; Press (ESC)" appears in the status line. Following the prompt the word requiring hyphenation is displayed with the suggested hyphenation. To accept the hyphenation as displayed, press (ESC). To change the hyphenation, move the hyphen with the arrow keys to the correct location and press (ESC). If the word cannot be appropriately hyphenated, press (F7) to cancel hyphenation for that word.

Hyphenating the newsletter has made the right margins much less ragged. Additionally, because more words were able to fit on a line, the last line of the first article now ends at the bottom of the first column, and the second article begins at the top of the second column. Karen is pleased with the appearance of the articles now.

Note: If your computer can display graphics, view the document again using **F**ile>**P**rint>View Document or Print (SHIFT) - (F7), **V**iew Document. To leave the View screen, press Exit (F7).

Move to the bottom of the second column and enter your name.
If you have printer capability, print a copy of the article. If necessary, select the appropriate printer for your microcomputer system first.

Saving and Exiting Two Document Files

When there are two documents in use, both need to be saved (if needed) and exited from before leaving the WordPerfect program. To save the current document,

Select: File>Exit
>> Exit (F7)
Type: Y
Type: COLUMNS.DOC
Press: ⏎

The next prompt, "Exit Doc 1?," is new. Whenever there are two open documents at one time, each document needs to be exited.

Type: Y

Document 2, the welcome letter, is displayed on the screen. Since no changes were made to this document, it is not necessary to save the file. To close this document and exit WordPerfect,

Select: File>Exit
>> Exit (F7)
Type: N
Type: Y

The DOS prompt appears on your display screen.

KEY TERMS

primary file	field	window
secondary merge file	record	underline
merge codes	center	newspaper columns
address file	boldface	parallel columns

MATCHING

1. End Record~ _____ a. boldfaces text
2. (SHIFT) - (F8) 2 _____ b. merges files
3. Field~ _____ c. displays merge codes
4. (F9) _____ d. identifies field name
5. (CTRL) - (F9) 1 _____ e. switches to other document
6. (SHIFT) - (F9) _____ f. displays Columns/Table menu
7. Layout>Align>Center _____ g. displays Page Format menu
8. (F6) _____ h. identifies end of field
9. (SHIFT) - (F3) _____ i. identifies end of record
10. (ALT) - (F7) _____ j. centers text

WORD PROCESSING

PRACTICE EXERCISES

1. You are the membership chairman of the Steady Striders Hiking Club, and you need to create a form letter to be sent out to new members. Follow the steps below to create this form letter.

    a. Create a secondary file. Each record will contain six fields of data. Name the fields appropriately and enter the following records:

        1. Janine
Allison
1330 Del Rosa Way
Sparks
NV
89434

        2. Danny
Clark
10730 Palm Springs
Sparks
NV
89436

        3. Nick
Turner
157 S. Maddux
Reno
NV
89512

    b. Save this secondary file as MEMBER.SF.

    c. Retrieve the file MEMBER (on your data diskette) and modify the letter to accept the six fields of information. Save the primary file as MEMBER.PF.

    d. Merge the primary and secondary files. Print all three letters. Save the merged file as MEMBER.MRG.

2. The Bumble Bee Lake Trail Building Club acknowledges supporters with a personalized thank-you letter. The form letter includes the following fields of data:

field 1	Firm
field 2	Name
field 3	Address
field 4	City
field 5	State-Zip
field 6	Contrib

shift F9, more

a. Create a secondary file using the following data for the records.

    1.   Hank's Hardware
         Hank
         2580 2nd Street
         Rancho Haven
         NV 89401
         shovels, rakes, and trash bags

    2.   Gerry's Sporting Goods
         Don
         3430 Old Canyon Road
         Carson City
         NV 89505
         gloves and trail markers

    3.   Alpine Mountain Deli
         Maureen
         200 W. Baker Street
         Reno
         NV 89512
         trail sandwiches for our volunteers

b. Save the secondary file as CONTRIB.SF.

c. Retrieve the file CONTRIB (on your data diskette).

d. Modify the thank-you letter by entering the appropriate merge codes to reflect the fields of data in the secondary merge file. *Type, shift F9*

e. Replace "Date" with the date code. Replace "[your name]" with your name in the closing.

f. Save the primary file as CONTRIB.PF on your data diskette and clear the screen.

g. Merge the primary and secondary files. Save the merged file as CONTRIB.MRG. Then print the letters. *F7, CTRL F9*

3. To complete this problem, you must first have completed Practice Exercise 1 in Lab 2. Retrieve the file CLOUDS.RPT.

Alt F4, CTRL F4

a. Delete the second and third paragraphs.

b. *shift F6* Center the title "CLOUD CLASSES and FOGS" on the first line of the document. Bold the title. Insert a blank line after the title. *F6*

c. Create two editing windows by splitting the screen. Set the first window to 11 lines. Switch to document 2 and retrieve the file FOG from your data diskette. *shift F3*   *CTRL F3 / Window   SHIFT F3*

d. *F8* Turn on the Underline feature. Center the title "FOG" on the first line of the document. Insert a blank line after the title. *shift F6*

e. *Alt F4, CTRL F4, shift F3, Enter* Copy the entire contents of document 2 to the end of document 1, between the text and your name and date. Separate the text with a blank line. Clear the window. Close document 2 without saving it. *F7, Y, Cloud Fog*   *CTRL F3, Wind, 24, Enter*   *F7, N, Y*

f. Enter and bold the titles "Cirrus," "Cumulus," and "Stratus" above the related paragraphs. Be sure a blank line separates each paragraph and title.

g. Change the text in document 1 to be displayed as three-column, newspaper-style columns. They should be separated by .4 inches.

h. Save the file as CLOUDFOG and print the document.

4. The Steady Striders Hiking Club is developing a trail guide about local animals that can be found in the Lake Tahini Basin. To see the information gathered so far, retrieve the file MAMMALS.

a. Center and bold the title "MAMMALS OF THE LAKE TAHINI BASIN."

b. Underline each of the animal names that precede the paragraphs.

c. Split the screen into two windows of 12 lines each. Switch to document 2 and retrieve the file SQUIRREL from your data diskette.

d. Underline each of the squirrels' names that precede the paragraphs.

e. Copy the text in document 2 into document 1, below the main title. Clear the window. Close document 2 without saving the changes.

f. Change the text in document 1 to be displayed as two-column, newspaper-style columns. They should be separated by .4 inches.

g. Save the file as MAMMALS and print the document.

5. The local Science Museum for Children acknowledges all gifts and donations with a personalized form letter that includes the following fields of data:

field 1	Full name
field 2	Street address
field 3	City
field 4	State
field 5	Zip code
field 6	Donation
field 7	Designation

a. Create a secondary merge file using the data shown below for each of the records.

1. Mr. and Mrs. Kevin Kelly
938 E. Flower Garden Way
East Aurora
NY
28193
$1,000
How Computers Work Exhibit

2. Mr. and Mrs. Brian White
371 W. Candlestick Parkway
Orchard Park
NY
27832
$2,500
Water Conservation Exhibit

3. Your first and last name
Street
City
State
Zip code
Donation
Designation

b. Save the secondary merge file as DONATION.SF.

c. The thank-you letter for donations is shown below. Create a primary file by entering this letter and the appropriate merge codes reflecting the fields of data in the secondary merge file.

[Date Command]

[Field 1]
[Field 2]
[Field 3], [Field 4] [Field 5]

Dear [Field 1]:

The Science Museum for Children would like to thank you for your generous donation of [Field 6]. As you specified, your donation will go toward the [Field 5].

The Science Museum for Children is continually building new exhibits and structures, renovating old structures and exhibits, and upgrading the museum grounds. It is through the generosity of donations such as yours that we are able to continue to improve and grow.

Your gift is greatly appreciated.

Development Director

d. Save the thank-you letter as DONATION.PF. Print the file.

e. Merge the primary and secondary files and print the letters.

LAB

Creating a Research Paper

4

OBJECTIVES

In this lab you will learn how to:

1. Create and edit an outline.

2. Draw lines.

3. Generate a table of contents.

4. Enter and edit footnotes.

5. Specify page numbering.

6. Suppress page numbering.

7. Center text top to bottom on a page.

8. Use Block Protection.

9. Prevent widows and orphans.

CASE STUDY

Peg is a senior recreation major at a local university. As part of her degree requirements she must work one semester in an approved internship program. To fulfill this requirement she worked at the Sports Club as an assistant in the swimming program.

As part of the requirements of the internship program, she must write a proposal on how to improve the swimming program. Her proposal is that the club offer an aquatic fitness program. In this lab we will follow Peg as she creates an outline and writes a paper on this topic.

Creating an Outline

Peg has already completed the research she needs and has thought about how the club could begin an aquatics fitness program. She needs to organize her thoughts and topics. To do this she decides to create an outline of the topics she plans to cover in her paper.

Boot the system and load the WordPerfect program.

The WordPerfect Automatic Outlining feature will help her prepare the outline for her proposal. This feature is accessed by selecting the Tools>Outline or Date/Outline (SHIFT) - (F5) command.

Note: If you use the function key command, the Date/Outline menu appears in the status line. The fourth option, Outline, then displays the Outline menu.

Select: **T**ools>**O**utline

>>   Date/Outline (SHIFT) - (F5), **O**utline

To turn on the Automatic Outlining feature,

Select: On

The WordPerfect screen is unchanged except for the message "Outline" displayed in the status line. This tells you that the Outline mode is on. WordPerfect will remain in this mode until you select this option again.

Peg has decided to divide her paper into three sections. In this lab you will learn how to create the outline for the first section of the paper as shown in Figure 4-1.

FIGURE 4-1

```
I.    Introduction

      A.    Statement of purpose
            1.    Justification for proposal
            2.    Organization of proposal
      B.    Reasons for aquatic exercise programs
            1.    Popularity of swimming
            2.    Benefits of aquatic exercise
                  a.    Adaptable to many people
                  b.    Less damaging to joints and bones
                  c.    Improves cardiovascular system
      C.    Determining Target Heart Rate (THR)
            1.    Define THR
            2.    Measure THR
                  a.    Direct
                  b.    Indirect
                        (1) Karvonen formula
                        (2) Percentage of Maximum Heart Rate (MHR)
```

In Outline mode the ⏎ and (TAB) keys perform specific functions. You will see how they perform differently as you create the outline. To begin outlining,

Press: ⏎

The Roman numeral "I." appears on the second line of the page. This is called a **paragraph number**. While in Outline mode the ⏎ key, in addition to inserting a blank line in the text, automatically displays a paragraph number. The Roman numeral I indicates that this is the first level of the outline.

To enter the text for the first line of the outline,

Press: Indent (F4)

The cursor has moved over one tab stop on the line. The Indent key ((F4)) moves the cursor along the line one tab stop. In normal text entry mode, the Indent key ((F4)) will align all text with the left tab stop until ⏎ is pressed. You may wonder why you did not use the (TAB) key to do this. As you will see shortly, the (TAB) key in Outline mode performs a different function.

To enter the text for this line,

Type: **Introduction**
Press: ⏎

Your screen should be similar to Figure 4-2.

paragraph number ——

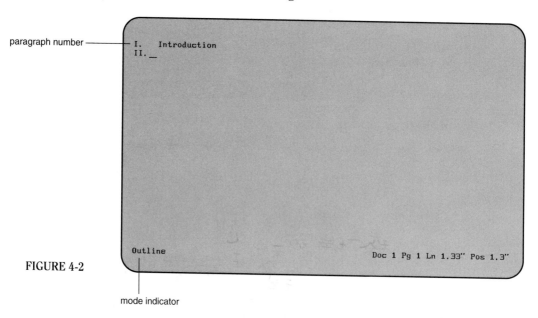

```
  I.    Introduction
 II. _




 Outline                                        Doc 1 Pg 1 Ln 1.33" Pos 1.3"
```

FIGURE 4-2

mode indicator

The Roman numeral "II." is displayed on the next line. Peg wants a blank line below the first outline level. Once a paragraph number is entered on a line, the ⏎ key can be used to insert a blank line.

Press: ⏎

A blank line is created, and Roman numeral II has moved down one line.

Next Peg needs to change the outline level from Roman numeral II to the second level of the outline, A. To do this,

Press: (TAB)

The cursor moved along the line one tab space, and "II." changed to "A." While outline mode is on, using (TAB) both changes the outline level number and tabs in one tab stop along the line.

Each time you press (TAB) the paragraph number advances to the next outline level. Instead of pressing (TAB), you could press Space bar five times to advance the cursor to the next tab stop, and the paragraph number would also automatically advance.

Note: If you press (TAB) too many times and find yourself in the wrong outline level, to back up a tab stop press Margin Release ((SHIFT) - (TAB)). The outline number will automatically adjust. If you press (BKSP) the automatic paragraph number for that line will be deleted. If that happens you will need to press ⏎ at the correct location to insert a new paragraph number.

To indent and enter the text for this level,

Press: (F4)
Type: **Statement of purpose**

WordPerfect inserts a hidden code in the outline at each tab location. These codes control the outline levels. To see the hidden paragraph number codes,

Select: **E**dit>**R**eveal Codes
   >>   Reveal Codes (ALT) - (F3)

Your screen should be similar to Figure 4-3.

FIGURE 4-3

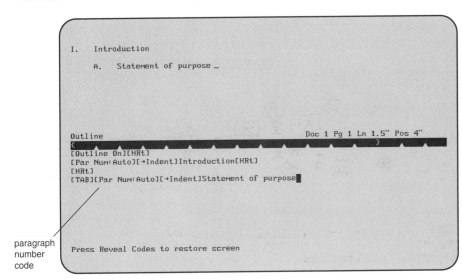

paragraph
number
code

The first code, [Outline On], was entered when you turned on the Automatic Outlining feature. The hidden code [Par Num:Auto] is automatically entered following a [TAB] or [HRt] code when in Outline mode. The number of tabs along the line determines the paragraph number level that is displayed in the outline. When you delete a [Par Num:Auto] code, the paragraph number disappears. To leave the Reveal Codes screen,

Select: **E**dit>**R**eveal Codes
   >>   Reveal Codes (ALT) - (F3)

     To continue the outline,

Press: (↵)

The new paragraph number is "B." When you press (↵) the new paragraph number is created at the same level as the previous number. In this case, however, the next line of the outline begins at the third level. To change the paragraph number to this level,

Press: (TAB)

The paragraph level number "1." is displayed. To indent and enter the text,

Press: Indent (F4)
Type: **Justification for proposal**
Press: (↵)

The paragraph number "2." appears on the line to allow you to enter the second topic at this outline level. Since this is the correct level for the next line of the outline, you are ready to enter the text for this level.

Press: Indent (F4)

Type: **Organization of proposal**

Press: (⏎)

A third-level paragraph number is displayed again. The next outline level to be entered is a second level. To change the level in the opposite direction, or to back up a level, Margin Release ((SHIFT) - (TAB)) is used. This is just the opposite of pressing (TAB) to increase the number's level.

Press: (SHIFT) - (TAB)

The outline number level has decreased one level and is now "B." To enter the text for this level,

Press: (F4)

Type: **Reasons for aquatic exercise programs**

Press: (⏎)

Complete the first section of the outline by entering the remaining outline levels as shown in Figure 4-4 using the (⏎), (TAB), (SHIFT) - (TAB), and Indent ((F4)) keys. Don't forget to indent before entering the text for each line. If you do forget to indent, you can use the cursor movement keys to move to the first character on the line and then press (F4). The editing and cursor movement keys can be used to correct the text in the outline in the same manner as in regular document entry.

When you are done your screen should be similar to Figure 4-4.

FIGURE 4-4

```
I.    Introduction

      A.    Statement of purpose
            1.    Justification for proposal
            2.    Organization of proposal
      B.    Reasons for aquatic exercise programs
            1.    Popularity of swimming
            2.    Benefits of aquatic exercise
                  a.    Adaptable to many people
                  b.    Less damaging to joints and bones
                  c.    Improves cardiovascular system
      C.    Determining Target Heart Rate (THR)
            1.    Define THR
            2.    Measure THR
                  a.    Direct
                  b.    Indirect
                        (1)  Karvonen formula
                        (2)  Percentage of Maximum Heart Rate_




Outline                                          Doc 1 Pg 1 Ln 4" Pos 6.7"
```

If you have not done so already, after typing the last line press (⏎).
To change the paragraph number to "II,"

Press: (SHIFT) - (TAB) (4 times)

To insert a blank line between section I and II of the outline,

Press: ⏎

The next two sections of the outline have already been completed for you and saved on the file OUTLINE1.W51. To combine the files, with your cursor positioned immediately after the "II.", retrieve the file OUTLINE1.W51.

The completed outline consists of three sections. The second topic area discusses the parts of an aquatic fitness routine. The third area discusses how an aquatic fitness program should be modified for people with different physical limitations. To see the complete outline use ⬇ to move to the end of the document.

Editing the Outline

After looking over her completed outline Peg wants to move a section of the outline to another location. It is easy to edit and move text within an outline while Outline mode is on. To move to the area of the outline that she wants to change,

Press : (HOME) - ⬆ (2 times)

Your screen should look similar to Figure 4-5.

FIGURE 4-5

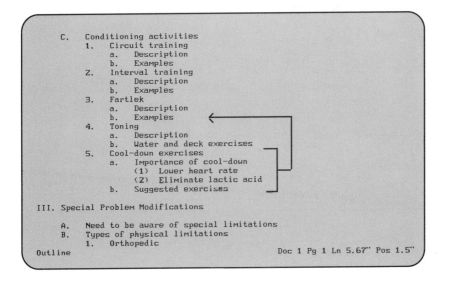

```
       C.    Conditioning activities
             1.    Circuit training
                   a.    Description
                   b.    Examples
             2.    Interval training
                   a.    Description
                   b.    Examples
             3.    Fartlek
                   a.    Description
                   b.    Examples
             4.    Toning
                   a.    Description
                   b.    Water and deck exercises
             5.    Cool-down exercises
                   a.    Importance of cool-down
                         (1)  Lower heart rate
                         (2)  Eliminate lactic acid
                   b.    Suggested exercises

  III. Special Problem Modifications

       A.    Need to be aware of special limitations
       B.    Types of physical limitations
             1.    Orthopedic
  Outline                                  Doc 1 Pg 1 Ln 5.67" Pos 1.5"
```

She wants to move the entire outline section "5. Cool-down exercises" above the section "4. Toning." She also wants to decrease the outline level of section 5 by one level, to level D.

Sections of an outline are grouped into **families**. A family consists of the outline level on the line where the cursor is located, plus any subordinate or lower levels. To move to the first line of the family to be moved,

Move to: Ln 7.83" Pos 1" (outline level "5. Cool-down exercises")
Select: Tools>Outline
   >>   Date/Outline (SHIFT) - (F5), **O**utline

Note: If you used the function key to issue this command, the outline menu will appear in the status line.

Your screen should be similar to Figure 4-6.

FIGURE 4-6

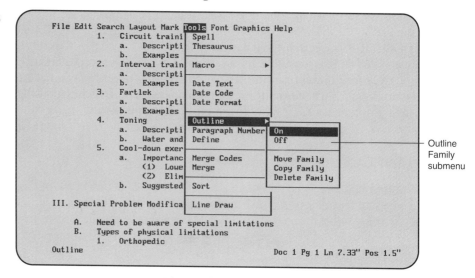

An outline family can be moved, copied, or deleted while in Outline mode using one of the three Family commands displayed in the submenu.

Select: Move Family

Outline level "5. Cool-down exercises" and the two sublevels below it should be highlighted. The highlighted outline family can be moved vertically or horizontally within the outline using the arrow keys.

Peg wants to move the family above the section of the outline beginning with "4. Toning." To move the outline family to this location,

Press:

Your screen should be similar to Figure 4-7.

FIGURE 4-7

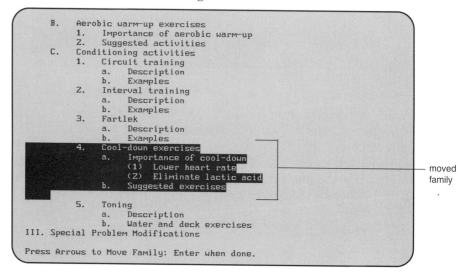

After a few seconds, the family moves up within the hierarchy of the outline and is now "4. Cool-down exercises," and the family below it has changed to "5. Toning."

Peg now wants to change the family from outline level 4 to level D. To do this, the paragraph number level needs to be lowered one level. Moving the highlighted family one level to the left will accomplish this task.

Press: ⟵

The outline family has moved one outline level to the left (horizontally), and all outline level numbers within the family have adjusted appropriately. Notice that the outline levels in the family below it have also adjusted. The new number, "3. Toning," however, is not how Peg wants it to be. She will correct this next.

To fix the highlighted family in place,

Press: ⏎

Next Peg wants to change the outline family beginning at level "3. Toning" to level E.

Move to: Ln 8.33" (outline level "3. Toning")
Select: **T**ools>**O**utline>**M**ove Family
  >> Date/Outline (SHIFT)-(F5), **O**utline>**M**ove Family

Press: ⟵
Press: ⏎

The family moved over one tab space on the line, and the paragraph number changed from "3." to "E." All sublevels below it have adjusted appropriately.

Finally, delete the blank line above this outline level by deleting the [HRt] following the word "Exercises" and add a blank line above outline level III. Be careful that you place the cursor correctly before deleting the line or pressing ⏎ to create a blank line. Use Reveal Codes to make sure you are deleting the correct codes.

Your screen should be similar to Figure 4-8.

FIGURE 4-8

```
        C.    Conditioning activities
              1.    Circuit training
                    a.    Description
                    b.    Examples
              2.    Interval training
                    a.    Description
                    b.    Examples
              3.    Fartlek
                    a.    Description
                    b.    Examples
        D.    Cool-down exercises
              1.    Importance of cool-down
                    a.    Lower heart rate
                    b.    Eliminate lactic acid
              2.    Suggested exercises
        E.    Toning
              1.    Description
              2.    Water and deck exercises

III.  Special Problem Modifications

        A.    Need to be aware of special limitations
        B.    Types of physical limitations
              1.    Orthopedic
Outline                              Doc 1 Pg 1 Ln 8.83" Pos 1.5"
```

WORD PROCESSING

This same task could be accomplished by deleting or adding [Tab] codes to reduce or increase the paragraph number level, and by using the Block feature to move sections of the outline. When using the Block feature to move a section of the outline, be careful to include all appropriate codes in the block, so that when it is moved the outline levels will adjust appropriately. However, the outline Family feature does the same thing more quickly and accurately. Use Block if the paragraphs you want to manipulate are not a family or if you are not in Outline mode.

Peg feels the outline will help her to organize the topics in her paper. To turn off Outline mode, place the cursor at the end of the outline, and then select Outline Off. To do this,

Press: (HOME) (HOME) (↓)
Select: **T**ools>**O**utline>Off
       >>   Date/Outline (SHIFT) - (F5), **O**utline>Off

The "Outline" indicator in the status line is no longer displayed indicating Outline mode is not on. An [Outline Off] code has been inserted into the document. Now you could continue typing normal text, and the (⏎) and (TAB) keys will act as they normally do. However, if you move the cursor into the area of text between the [Outline on] and [Outline Off] codes, the (⏎) and (TAB) keys will work as they do in Outline mode.

Peg wants to enter a centered title at the beginning of the outline. To do this,

Press: (PGUP)
Press: Center (SHIFT) - (F6)
Type: **OUTLINE FOR AQUATIC FITNESS PROPOSAL**
Press: (⏎)

On the next line center your name and the current date.
To separate the two title lines from the beginning of the outline,

Press: (⏎) (2 times)

Your screen should be similar to Figure 4-9.

FIGURE 4-9

```
                OUTLINE FOR AQUATIC FITNESS PROPOSAL
                     Student Name    Date

     ‾
   I.   Introduction

        A.   Statement of purpose
             1.   Justification for proposal
             2.   Organization of proposal
        B.   Reasons for aquatic exercise programs
             1.   Popularity of swimming
             2.   Benefits of aquatic exercise
                  a.   Adaptable to many people
                  b.   Less damaging to joints and bones
                  c.   Improves cardiovascular system
        C.   Determining Target Heart Rate (THR)
             1.   Define THR
             2.   Measure THR
                  a.   Direct
                  b.   Indirect
                       (1)  Karvonen formula
                       (2)  Percentage of Maximum Heart Rate

   II.  Aquatic Fitness Routine
                                         Doc 1 Pg 1 Ln 1.33" Pos 1"
```

Using Save (F10), save the outline as OUTLINE2.

Print the outline. If necessary select the printer that is appropriate for your computer system.

Clear the screen (Exit (F7)). Do not exit WordPerfect.

Creating Lines

After several days, Peg has written the body of the internship proposal using WordPerfect 5.1 and has saved it on the diskette as PROPOSAL.W51.

To see what she has done so far, retrieve PROPOSAL.W51.

The title page of the report should be displayed on your screen. The first thing Peg would like to do is to draw a line below the title of the report. WordPerfect's Line Draw feature lets you draw lines, boxes, graphs, and other illustrations in your document. The Line Draw feature is an option that is accessed through the Tools menu or (CTRL) - (F3).

Select: Tools>Line Draw
>>   Screen (CTRL) - (F3), Line Draw

Your screen should be similar to Figure 4-10.

FIGURE 4-10

```
  —




                    A PROGRAM IN

                    AQUATIC FITNESS

                    FOR THE SPORTS CLUB







 1 |; 2 ||; 3 *; 4 Change; 5 Erase; 6 Move: 1          Ln 1" Pos 1"
```

The Line Draw menu is displayed in the status line. This menu lets you create a single line (1), double line (2), or a line composed of asterisks (3). Change, option 4, lets you change the style of option 3 to something other than an asterisk from a selection of choices. The default is a single line.

Lines are created by using the arrow keys. Once this menu is displayed the arrow keys will automatically begin creating a line if they are pressed. To move the cursor without creating a line, the Move option (6) must be selected. Since Peg wants to create a line below the title, she needs to move the cursor to the line and position where the line is to begin. To do this,

Select: Move

The Line Draw menu is still displayed. Following the colon at the end of the menu, the selected option is displayed. Now the cursor can be moved without creating a line. She wants the line to be two lines below the last line of the title. Using the arrow keys,

Move to: Ln 2.83" Pos 2.6"

Peg wants to create a double line. To do this,

Select: 2

The menu remains on the screen, with the selected option, 2, displayed following the colon in the menu.
To create the line, using the ⊖ key,

Move to: Ln 2.83" Pos 6.5"

Your screen should be similar to Figure 4-11.

FIGURE 4-11

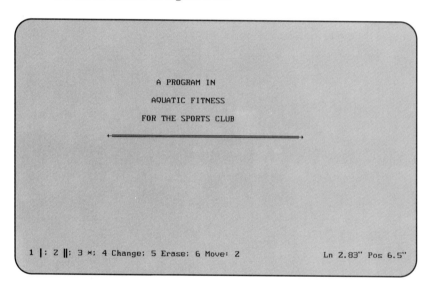

```
                    A PROGRAM IN

                   AQUATIC FITNESS

                  FOR THE SPORTS CLUB

  ◄═══════════════════════════════════════►




  1 |: 2 ||: 3 ×; 4 Change; 5 Erase; 6 Move: 2          Ln 2.83" Pos 6.5"
```

The line has been created. However, Peg thinks the line is too long. The Erase menu option will let you erase a line or a part of a line.

Select: Erase

To delete part of the line, using ⊖,

Move to: Ln 2.83" Pos 5.8"

The line is shortened. To turn off the Line Draw feature,

Press: Exit (F7)

You are returned to the document, and the Line Draw menu is no longer displayed.

After looking at the title, Peg thinks that another line above the title would look good.

Move to:	Ln 1.5" Pos 2.6" (Use Space bar to move to Pos 2.6")
Select:	**T**ools>**L**ine Draw
>>	Screen (CTRL) - (F3), **L**ine Draw

This time she wants to create a single line.

| **Select:** | 1 |
| **Move to:** | Ln 1.5" Pos 5.8" |

Peg is happy with how the line appears and does not want to make any other changes. To leave the Line Draw feature,

| **Press:** | **Exit** (F7) |

When the lines are printed the arrows at the beginning and end of the lines will not be printed.

Complete the title page by entering "By your name" on line 5.67". On line 5.83" enter the title of the course, and on the next line enter the current date as code using the Date command (Tools>Date Code or (SHIFT) - (F5), Date Code). All three lines should be centered on the page.

Creating a Table of Contents

Next Peg needs to create a table of contents for the report. Using ⓓ,

| **Move to:** | Pg 2 Ln 1.5" |

The second page of the report contains the heading "TABLE OF CONTENTS" centered on the page. The table of contents can be generated automatically by WordPerfect from text within the document. There are three steps to creating a table of contents:

Step 1   The text to be used in the table of contents is marked.
Step 2   The location where the table is to be displayed is specified.
Step 3   The table is generated or created.

Step 1: Marking Text for the Table of Contents

The Mark menu, or Mark Text (ALT) - (F5), marks the text to be used in the table of contents. Before selecting the command you must first highlight the text to be used as the table of contents heading.

The first heading to be marked is "INTRODUCTION." To move to the top of page 3,

| **Press:** | (PGDN) |

When a block is defined that will be used in a table of contents, any codes that are included in the block will be included in the table of contents when it is created. Since this heading is in bold and centered, if the [Center] and [BOLD] codes are also included when the block is defined, the heading in the table of contents will appear both boldfaced and centered. Therefore you must be careful when highlighting a block of text to include in a table of contents, that only the codes you want are specified.

To display the codes while blocking the text,

Select: File>**R**eveal Codes
>>   Reveal Codes (ALT) - (F3)

The cursor is positioned on the [Center] code, as you can see in the Reveal Codes portion of the window. Peg does not want to include either the [BOLD] code or the [Center] code in the block. To move the cursor to the right of the codes,

Press: (CTRL) - (→)

The cursor should be on the "I" in "INTRODUCTION." Next you need to highlight the word "INTRODUCTION," which will be used in the table of contents. While in Reveal Codes screen you can use the Block feature to highlight text; or you can use the mouse.

To turn on the Block feature,

Select: **E**dit>**B**lock
>>   Block (ALT) - (F4)

"Block on" flashes in the status line of the upper part of the window, and a [Block] code is displayed in the Reveal Codes area. To highlight "INTRODUCTION,"

Press: (→) (12 times) or drag the mouse

Your screen should be similar to Figure 4-12.

FIGURE 4-12

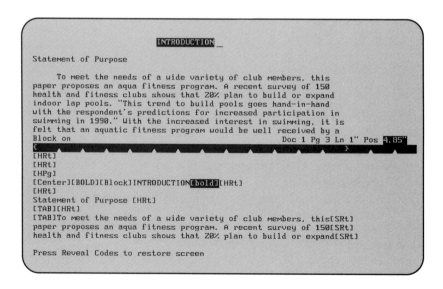

"INTRODUCTION" is highlighted in the upper screen, and the cursor is positioned on the ending [bold] code in the Reveal Codes screen. None of the codes surrounding the text will be included in the block.

To leave the Reveal Codes screen,

Select: Edit>Reveal Codes
>> Reveal Codes (ALT) - (F3)

The Block On feature should still be active.

Next, to tell WordPerfect that this block of text is to be used in a table of contents, it must be marked. The Mark menu, or Mark Text (ALT) - (F5), lets you specify the type of text you want to identify.

Select: Mark
>> Mark Text (ALT) - (F5)

Your screen should be similar to Figure 4-13. (If you used the function key command (ALT) - (F5) the menu is displayed in the status line.)

FIGURE 4-13

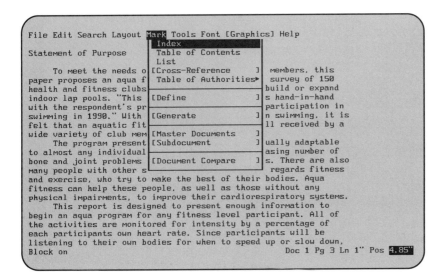

As you can see from the menu, text can also be marked to create a list, an index, a cross reference, or a table of authorities. The ToC option will mark a block for use in a table of contents by placing a [Mark] code at the beginning of the block and an [End Mark] code at the end of the block of text.

Select: Table of Contents
>> ToC

The prompt "ToC Level:" is displayed.

A table of contents can have up to five levels of heads. The selection of the level of heads determines how the table of contents will look. A **level one head** is the main head. A blank line is placed before all first-level entries. The **level two head** is subordinate to the

Creating a
Research Paper

level one head and is not separated from it by blank lines. Level two heads appear indented under the level one head. For example:

> This is a level one head.
>> This is a level two subhead.
>> This is a level two subhead.

> This is a level one head.
>> This is a level two subhead.

Peg wants to create a table of contents that will display the three main topics (I, II, and III in the outline) as level one heads. To identify the blocked text as a level one head,

Type: 1
Press: ⏎

You are returned to the document. The heading "INTRODUCTION" has been marked to be part of the table of contents.

The next heading to be marked is "Statement of Purpose" on line 1.33". Since there are no codes surrounding this block of text, you can simply highlight the block. This heading will be a second-level head in the table of contents.

Move to: Pg 3 Ln 1.33" Pos 1" (on "S" in "Statement")
Select: **Edit>Block**
>>   **Block** (ALT) - (F4)

Highlight "Statement of Purpose". The cursor should be on Pos 3".

Then, to mark the text as a second-level head in the table of contents,

Select: **Mark>Table of Contents**
>>   Mark Text (ALT) - (F5), ToC
Type: 2
Press: ⏎

To see the hidden codes marking the text for level one and level two table of contents heads,

Select: **Edit>Reveal Codes**
>>   Reveal Codes (ALT) - (F3)

Your screen should be similar to Figure 4-14.

FIGURE 4-14

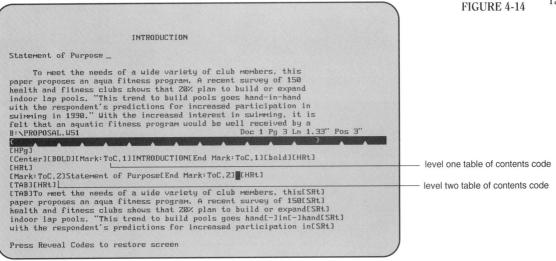

level one table of contents code

level two table of contents code

The mark text codes are displayed surrounding the text to be used in the table of contents. The two levels are also differentiated within the codes. If you needed to delete a table of contents heading, you would simply delete the code surrounding the text.

To return to the document,

Select: Edit>Reveal Codes

>> Reveal Codes (ALT) - (F3)

Mark the next two headings as level two table of contents heads. They are:

Reasons for Aquatic Exercise Program - Pg 3 Ln 6.5"
Determining Target Heart Rate (THR) - Pg 4 Ln 1.83"

Next mark AQUATIC FITNESS ROUTINE (Pg 5 Ln 8") as a level one table of contents head. Be careful not to include the center and bold codes when blocking the heading.

Finally, mark the next two headings as level two table of contents heads:

Warm-up Stretches - Pg 6 Ln 1"
Aerobic Warm-up Exercises - Pg 6 Ln 4.67"

Note: You will complete marking the remaining table of contents heads in a practice exercise at the end of this lab.

Step 2: Define Table of Contents Location

The second step is to define where the table of contents is to be inserted into the document.

Move to: Pg 2 Ln 1.5" Pos 1" (3 lines below the heading "TABLE OF CONTENTS")

The Mark menu (or (ALT) - (F5)) option Define lets you specify the location for the table.

Select: **M**ark>**D**efine
>>   Mark Text (ALT) - (F5), **D**efine

Your screen should be similar to Figure 4-15.

FIGURE 4-15

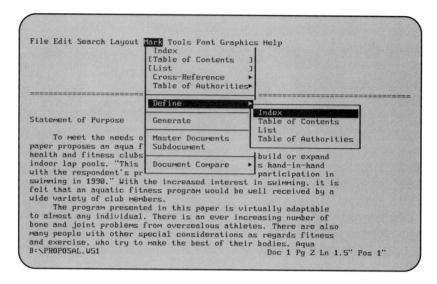

Note: If you used the function key to issue this command, the document is replaced by a full-screen menu of five options. They are the same choices which are available in the Define submenu.

Select: Table of **C**ontents
>>   Define Table of **C**ontents

Your screen should be similar to Figure 4-16.

FIGURE 4-16

```
Table of Contents Definition

    1 - Number of Levels          1

    Z - Display Last Level in     No
          Wrapped Format

    3 - Page Numbering - Level 1  Flush right with leader
                         Level 2
                         Level 3
                         Level 4
                         Level 5











Selection: 0
```

A full-screen menu is displayed. This is the Table of Contents Definition menu. Option 1 Number of Levels displays the default setting of 1 as the number of levels used in the table of contents. Since you defined two levels in the table of contents, change this setting to 2.

Select: Number of Levels
Type: 2

The second option lets you specify whether you want the second-level entries to wrap, or to each be displayed on a separate line. You want each level to be displayed on a separate line. This is the default, and requires no adjustment.

The third option lets you select the page numbering style for each level. The default will display the page numbers flush with the right side of the page with a series of dots, or **leaders**, between the header and the page number. To select this option,

Select: **P**age Numbering

The five numbering styles are displayed in the status line. To leave the page numbering style as it is for both levels and to exit this menu,

Press: Exit (F7)

To leave the Table of Contents Definition menu,

Press: (↵)

You are returned to the document. To see the codes,

Select: **E**dit>**R**eveal Codes
  >> Reveal Codes (ALT) - (F3)

The code [Def Mark ToC,2:5,5] has been entered into the document at this location. This code will tell WordPerfect where to place the table of contents when it is generated.

Select: **E**dit>**R**eveal Codes
  >> Reveal Codes (ALT) - (F3)

Step 3: Generate the Table of Contents

Finally, you are ready for WordPerfect to do a little work. Once all the headings are marked and the table of contents definitions completed, the table of contents can be generated.

Select: **M**ark>**G**enerate
  >> Mark Text (ALT) - (F5), **G**enerate

The Mark Text: Generate menu is displayed. To generate the table of contents,

Select: **G**enerate Tables, Index, Cross-References, etc.

The prompt at the bottom of the screen asks you to confirm that you want any existing tables deleted. Since there are no other tables created in this document, you can accept the default response of Yes.

Type: Y

The message displayed at the bottom of the screen tells you that generation has started. The "Pass:" and "Page:" indicators help you keep track of its progress. When complete the table of contents should be displayed.

Your screen should be similar to Figure 4-17.

FIGURE 4-17

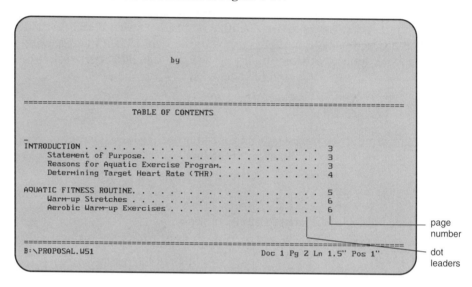

page number

dot leaders

The table of contents for the first few pages of the report is displayed. A blank line separates the first-level heads. The level two heads appear indented under the level one heads. The page numbers are displayed flush with the right side of the page. A series of dots, or leaders, separates the heads from the page numbers, as specified.

Creating Footnotes

Next Peg needs to enter footnotes into her paper. WordPerfect can help her do this by automatically numbering the footnotes and placing them properly at the bottom of the page. The Footnote (Layout>Footnote or Footnote (CTRL) - (F7), 1) command is used to create footnotes.

Before using the Footnote command, the cursor must be positioned in the text where the footnote number is to be inserted. Peg's first footnote will appear following the quote in the first paragraph of the Statement of Purpose on page 3.

Press: (PGDN)

Move to: Ln 2.5" Pos 2.8" (after the quotes (") on the sixth line of the first paragraph of page 3)

Select: Layout

>>   Footnote (CTRL) - (F7)

The Layout menu options, Footnote and Endnote (displayed in the status line if you used the function key), let you create and edit footnotes or endnotes. The procedure for both is very similar. The difference is that footnotes are printed at the bottom of the page where the reference is made, and endnotes are compiled as a list at the end of the document.

To create a footnote,

Select: Footnote

Your screen should be similar to Figure 4-18.

FIGURE 4-18

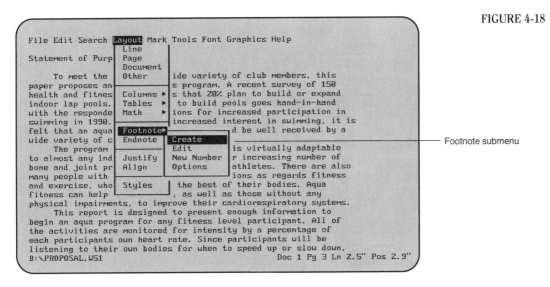

Footnote submenu

The four Footnote submenu options (displayed in the status line if you used the function key command) let you create and edit footnotes. To create a footnote,

Select: Create

The text has been replaced by a nearly blank screen. This is a special editing screen used to enter the text for the endnote or footnote. The note can be up to 16,000 lines long. The number 1 displayed on the screen shows that this is the first footnote entered in the text.

To enter a space after the number and before the text of the footnote,

Press: Space bar

When entering a footnote, the same commands and features you use in the normal document editing can be used.

Type: "Participation Up, Swimming Forecast Looks Strong," Athletic Business, July 1988, p. 37. (Do not press ⏎)

Your screen should be similar to Figure 4-19.

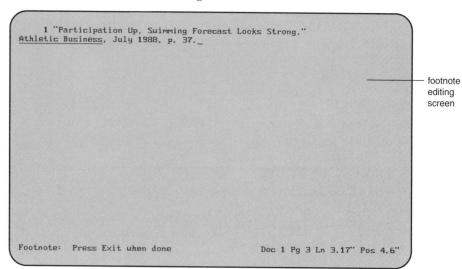

footnote
editing
screen

FIGURE 4-19

```
    1 "Participation Up, Swimming Forecast Looks Strong,"
Athletic Business, July 1988, p. 37._




















Footnote:   Press Exit when done                    Doc 1 Pg 3 Ln 3.17" Pos 4.6"
```

To save the footnote and return to the document,

Press: Exit (F7)

Your screen should be similar to Figure 4-20.

footnote number

FIGURE 4-20

```
                        INTRODUCTION

Statement of Purpose

      To meet the needs of a wide variety of club members, this
paper proposes an aqua fitness program. A recent survey of 150
health and fitness clubs shows that 20% plan to build or expand
indoor lap pools. "This trend to build pools goes hand-in-hand
with the respondent's predictions for increased participation in
swimming in 1990."1 With the increased interest in swimming, it
is felt that an aquatic fitness program would be well received by
a wide variety of club members.
      The program presented in this paper is virtually adaptable
to almost any individual. There is an ever increasing number of
bone and joint problems from overzealous athletes. There are also
many people with other special considerations as regards fitness
and exercise, who try to make the best of their bodies. Aqua
fitness can help these people, as well as those without any
physical impairments, to improve their cardiorespiratory systems.
      This report is designed to present enough information to
begin an aqua program for any fitness level participant. All of
the activities are monitored for intensity by a percentage of
each participants own heart rate. Since participants will be
listening to their own bodies for when to speed up or slow down,
B:\PROPOSAL.WS1                               Doc 1 Pg 3 Ln 2.5" Pos 2.9"
```

The footnote number, 1, is entered in the text at the location of the cursor. On some screens it may appear highlighted or superscripted. It will appear as a superscript number when printed. The footnotes will not appear on the screen. When the page or entire report is printed, they will be automatically printed on the bottom of the page containing the footnote number.

To enter the second footnote,

Move to: Pg 3 Ln 8.67" Pos 4.8" (space after "water." on third line of sixth
paragraph)

Select: Layout>Footnote>Create
    >> Footnote (CTRL) - (F7), Footnote>Create

Notice that the footnote number on the screen is 2.

Press: Space bar
Type: **President's Council on Physical Fitness and Sports, <u>Aqua Dynamics:</u>**
            <u>Physical Conditioning Through Water Exercises</u>, p. 1.
Press: **Exit** (F7)

The second footnote number is entered in the text.
    Peg forgot to enter a footnote earlier in the text.

Move to: Pg 3 Ln 7.33" Pos 6.8" (space after the word "activity." on fourth line of
                            fifth paragraph)
Select: Layout>Footnote>Create
    >> Footnote (CTRL) - (F7), Footnote>Create

Notice that this footnote is number 2. WordPerfect automatically adjusted the footnote numbers when the new footnote was inserted.

Press: Space bar
Type: **Ibid.**
Press: **Exit** (F7)

Notice that both footnotes are still displayed as footnote 2. To update the screen
display using the Rewrite feature,

Select: Screen (CTRL) - (F3), **R**ewrite
Move to: Pg 4 Ln 1"

Your screen should be similar to Figure 4-21.

FIGURE 4-21

```
participants will learn to monitor their own heart rates and work
at their own intensity levels.
    There is also a section on some special modifications for
people with some physical limitations. Almost all people should
be encouraged to participate aerobically in a way that is safe
for them. Aqua fitness is a safe, fun, and smart step toward
cardiovascular wellness.

Reasons for Aquatic Exercise Program

    Cardiorespiratory or "aerobic" form of exercise is one of                        ——— footnote 2
the most popular activities in the United States. Currently,
swimming is the sixth most popular club activity. By 1990 it is
expected that it will be the fourth most popular activity.2 There
are many forms of aerobic exercises: jogging, aerobic classes,
and swimming are just a few. What they have in common is the
ability to raise the heart rate over a period of time. This
report will explore the benefits of an aquatic aerobics exercise
program.
    Exercises can be performed more easily in the water because
of the lessening effect of gravitation. Approximately 90% of your                    ——— page break
_____
body weight is supported by the water.3 A person weighing 130
pounds immersed in the water only has to support 13 pounds. This
B:\PROPOSAL.WS1                        Doc 2 Pg 4 Ln 1" Pos 6.9"                       ——— footnote 3
```

The footnote number for the third footnote changed to 3. Also notice that the sentence containing the third footnote moved to the top of page 4. This is because WordPerfect determined there would not be enough space at the bottom of page 3 to display two footnotes and the associated text.

Editing a Footnote

Peg realizes that she forgot to enter the date in the footnote text for the third footnote. The Edit option in the Footnote submenu lets you change the information in an existing footnote. To edit a footnote you can be anywhere within the document. To edit footnote 3,

Select: Layout>Footnote>Edit
  >>   Footnote (CTRL) - (F7), Footnote>Edit

The prompt to enter the number of the footnote that you want to edit is displayed. If the correct footnote number is displayed following the prompt you can press (⏎) to accept it. Otherwise you must type in the footnote number following the prompt. Since you want to edit footnote number 3,

Type: 3
Press: (⏎)

The text for footnote 3 is displayed on the screen. To add the date before the page number of the footnote,

Move to: Ln 1.67" Pos 6.7"
Type: 1981,
Press: Space bar
Press: Exit (F7)

Now Peg wants to see how the page containing the footnotes will appear when printed. To see how the footnotes on page 3 will appear when printed move to anywhere within page 3, then

Select: File>Print> View Document
  >>   Print (SHIFT) - (F7), View Document

After a few moments page 3 is generated and displayed in the View Document screen.

Note: If your computer does not have graphics capabilities, your screen cannot display the entire page. Instead it will display the first 24 lines of the page with the margins and other print options as close as possible to how it will appear when printed. The instructions that follow do not apply to your computer system. Instead, to see the footnotes as they will appear when printed, press (CTRL) - (HOME) (↓). The footnotes will appear as they will be printed; however, the footnote numbers will not appear in super-script. To leave the View screen, press F7. Continue the lab by skipping to the next section, "Numbering Pages."

If you are not viewing the bottom of the page and your View screen is not 100%,

Select: 1 100%
Press: HOME ↓

The text is large enough to read easily. Notice that the footnote number is displayed in superscript, and the footnotes appear at the bottom of the page as they will be printed.

To leave the View screen,

Press: Exit F7

Numbering Pages

Next Peg wants to instruct WordPerfect to print page numbers for each page in the report. The code to create page numbering is entered on the page where you want page numbering to begin. Generally this is the beginning of the document. To move to the top of page 1,

Press: HOME HOME ↑

The Layout>Page, or Format (SHIFT) - F8, Page, command is used to specify page numbering.

Select: Layout>Page
   >>   Format (SHIFT) - F8, Page

The Page Format menu is displayed. The Page Numbering option lets you specify the placement of numbers on the pages.

Select: Page Numbering

The Format: Page Numbering menu is displayed. The four options let you control how and where page numbers are inserted. To turn on page numbering from the cursor position forward, you need to specify where you want the page number placed on the page. The Page Number Position option shows the default is to display no page numbers. To change this setting and specify where you want the number placed,

Select: Page Number Position

Your screen should be similar to Figure 4-22.

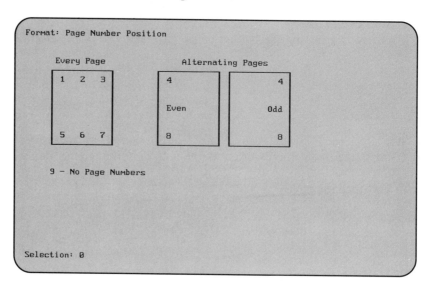

FIGURE 4-22

The Format: Page Number Position menu is displayed. The numbers displayed on the page layout let you specify where the page number will appear. The option number corresponds to its position on the page layout. Peg wants each page number centered on the bottom of every page (option 6),

Select: 6

The new page number position, bottom center, is displayed. To return to the document,

Press: Exit (F7)

The page numbers will not appear on the screen. However, when the document is printed the page numbers will appear on the margin of the location specified. If new pages are inserted or others deleted, WordPerfect will automatically renumber the pages.

Suppressing Page Numbers

Peg realizes that she really does not want the title and table of contents pages to be numbered. She can turn off the page numbering for specified pages using the Page Format menu. To do this, the cursor must be positioned at the beginning of the page to be unnumbered.

The cursor should already be on the first line of page 1. If it is not, move it there.

Select: Layout>Page
>> Format (SHIFT) - (F8), Page

The option "Suppress (this page only)" will turn off page numbering for the page the cursor is on.

Select: Suppress (this page only)

Your screen should be similar to Figure 4-23.

FIGURE 4-23

```
Format: Suppress (this page only)

    1 - Suppress All Page Numbering, Headers and Footers

    2 - Suppress Headers and Footers

    3 - Print Page Number at Bottom Center    No

    4 - Suppress Page Numbering              No

    5 - Suppress Header A                    No

    6 - Suppress Header B                    No

    7 - Suppress Footer A                    No

    8 - Suppress Footer B                    No




Selection: 0
```

A menu of eight options is displayed. The options allow you to suppress or temporarily turn off different page format settings. To turn off page numbering and return to the document,

Select: Suppress **P**age Numbering
Type: Y
Press: Exit (F7)

Use the Reveal Codes screen to look at the codes inserted at this location in your document. It should display [Pg Numbering:Bottom Center][Suppress:PgNum]. Exit the Reveal Codes screen.

Following the procedure above, suppress the page numbering for the Table of Contents page (page 2).

Centering Text Top to Bottom

Next Peg would like the text on the title page to be centered between top and bottom margins of the page. Before this command is used the cursor needs to be positioned at the top left margin of the page to be centered.

Press: (HOME) (HOME) (↑)

The cursor should be on the left margin of the first line of page 1. The Center Page option (1) in the Page Format menu will automatically center the text vertically on a page.

Select:	Layout>Page
>>	Format (SHIFT) - (F8), **Page**
Select:	Center Page (top to bottom)
Type:	**Y**
Press:	Exit (F7)

Again, not until you print or view the page will you see how the text is centered on the page. It will position the text on this page so that an equal number of blank lines lie above and below the first and last line of text.

Center the text on the table of contents page. Use the Reveal Codes screen to view the codes entered at this location.

Using Block Protection

Peg has one last concern. She wants to make sure that text that should remain together on one page, such as a table or a long quote, is not divided over two pages. This situation frequently occurs because WordPerfect automatically calculates the length of each page and inserts a **soft page break** when needed without discrimination as to the text. The position of a soft page break will change as text is added or deleted.

To control where a page ends you could enter a **hard page break** to make WordPerfect begin a new page. A hard page break is entered by pressing (CTRL) - (↵). However, if you continue to edit the document by adding and deleting text that affects the length of the document, the location of the hard page break may no longer be appropriate. Then you would need to delete the hard page break code and reenter it at the new location. To do this is time consuming.

One solution is to use the Block Protection command (Edit>Protect Block or Block (ALT) - (F4), Format (SHIFT) - (F8)) to keep a specified block of text together on a page. Before using Block Protection, the block of text must be marked. The area of text which Peg does not want to be split between two pages is on page 5.

Move to:	Pg 5 Ln 1.5" Pos 1" ("W" in "With")

To specify the first block of text to protect,

Select:	Edit>Block
>>	Block (ALT) - (F4)

Highlight the text on lines 1.5" through 2.33". The highlight should cover the lead-in sentence and the following three lines of formulas.

Select:	Edit>Protect Block

To see the hidden codes entered into the text as a result of using this command,

Select: **E**dit>**R**eveal Codes
     >>   Reveal Codes (ALT) - (F3)
Press: (↑) (2 times)

Your screen should be similar to Figure 4-24.

FIGURE 4-24

```
is estimated by subtracting the participant's age from 220.
Participants should supply their RHR, which should be taken in
the morning, ideally before they get up and start moving around.
With this information the formula is used like this:

    MHR = 220 - AGE
    HRR = MHR - RHR
_   THR = HRR (60-80%) + RHR

For example, the THR for a person 29 years old with an RHR of 62
and a desired intensity of 70% is calculated as follows:
B:\PROPOSAL.W51                              Doc 1 Pg 5 Ln 2" Pos 1"
‹                                            ›
[Block Pro:On]With this information the formula is used like this:[HRt]
[HRt]
[TAB]MHR = 220 [-] AGE[HRt]
[TAB]HRR = MHR [-] RHR[HRt]
[TAB]THR = HRR (60[-]80%) + RHR[HRt]
[Block Pro:Off][HRt]
For example, the THR for a person 29 years old with an RHR of 62[SRt]
and a desired intensity of 70% is calculated as follows:[HRt]
[HRt]
[TAB]MHR = 220 [-] 29        MHR = 191[HRt]

Press Reveal Codes to restore screen
```
— Block Protect code

A [Block Pro:On] code is inserted at the beginning of the block, and a [Block Pro:Off] code is inserted at the end of the block. Now, when WordPerfect formats this page for printing, the text between these codes will never be divided between two pages. If there is not enough space on a page to accommodate the entire block of text a page break is inserted above the [Block Pro:On] code, and the entire block is moved to the next page.

However, in this case it appears that there are enough lines left on this page to keep the entire block of text together, and no page break is inserted. It is always a good idea to turn on Block Protection even though it currently may appear that it is not needed. Later editing of the document may change the location of the block in the text, resulting in a split between two pages.

To remove the Reveal Codes screen,

Select: **E**dit>**R**eveal Codes
     >>   Reveal Codes (ALT) - (F3)

The next block to be protected begins on Pg 5 Ln 2.5" through Ln 3.33". This block begins with the words "For example" and ends after the third line of formulas. Block this area of text.

To protect this block, you will use the function key equivalent this time. It is (SHIFT) - (F8).

Select: Format (SHIFT) - (F8)

The prompt "Protect Block?" appears in the status line. To turn on protection,

Type: Y

As Peg looks through the document she notices that a chart which begins on page 5 is divided between two pages. To move to the bottom of page 5,

Press: CTRL - HOME ↓

As you can see, the fitness table which begins on page 5 continues on page 6. Following the above procedure, protect the table and lead-in sentence (beginning with the word "Once") to prevent the text from appearing on separate pages. (The block should extend through Pg 6 Ln 1.5".)

Your screen should be similar to Figure 4-25.

FIGURE 4-25

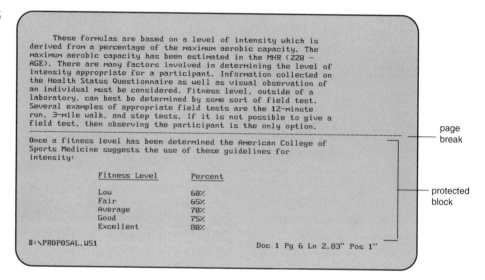

This time a page break is inserted by the program so that the entire block begins on the following page. Using Block Protection Peg could add more lines of data within the block codes, and the protection would remain in effect.

Preventing Widows and Orphans

The second way to control how text is divided between two pages is to turn on Widow/Orphan Protection. When the first line of a paragraph is the last line on a page it is called a **widow**. When the last line of a paragraph appears at the top of a new page it is called an **orphan**. To prevent this type of problem from occurring, the Widow/Orphan Protection command is used.

The Widow/Orphan Protection command (Layout>Line>Widow/Orphan Protection or SHIFT - F8, Line>Widow/Orphan Protection) should be entered at the beginning of the document so that all the following text will be affected. To move back to the beginning of the document and to use this command,

Press: (HOME) (HOME) (↑)
Select: **Layout>Line**
>> Format (SHIFT) - (F8), Line

The Line Format menu is displayed. The last option, 9, Widow/Orphan, will turn on this protection.

Select: **W**idow/Orphan Protection

The cursor moved to the default for this option. To turn on Widow/Orphan Protection,

Type: **Y**
Press: Exit (F7)

To see the hidden codes,

Select: **E**dit>**R**eveal Codes
>> Reveal Codes (ALT) - (F3)

Your screen should be similar to Figure 4-26.

FIGURE 4-26

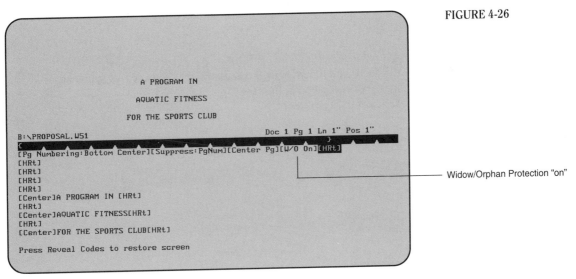

Widow/Orphan Protection "on"

The four page-format codes you entered at the beginning of the document are displayed. The code [W/O on] will will automatically determine when it is necessary to adjust the text on a page to eliminate widows and orphans. This protection applies only to traditional paragraphs, however.

Select: **E**dit>**R**eveal Codes
>> Reveal Codes (ALT) - (F3)

Printing the Report

Although Peg has a lot more work to do on the report, she wants to print out the first few pages of the text to see how the page settings and footnotes will appear.

Select: **File>Print**
     >>   Print (SHIFT) - (F7)

Next select the printer you want to use to print this document.
     The option Multiple Pages will let you specify which pages of the on-screen document to print.

Select: Multiple Pages

The prompt "Page(s):" allows you to print the entire document (All), which is the default, individual pages, or any range of pages.

     To print pages 1 through 3, 5, and 6,

Type: **1-3,5,6**
Press: ⏎

The prompt "Document may need to be generated. Print?" is displayed. In response to this prompt,

Type: **Y**

The specified pages should be printing.
     Check to see that the page numbers are displayed as specified, that the first two pages are centered, and that the footnotes are correct.
     To leave the Print menu,

Press: ⏎

Save the edited report as FITNESS and exit WordPerfect.

Key Terms

paragraph number
family
level one head
level two head
leader
soft page break
hard page break
widow
orphan

Matching

1. (SHIFT) - (F5), 4 _____ **a.** allows you to specify the placement of page numbers
2. [Par Num:Auto] _____ **b.** turns on the Outline feature
3. (CTRL) - (F3), 3 _____ **c.** reformats the display of the screen
4. (ALT) - (F5),1, 2 _____ **d.** the View Document command
5. (ALT) - (F5), 6 _____ **e.** the code for an outline paragraph number
6. (CTRL) - (F7), 1 _____ **f.** creates a footnote
7. (CTRL) - (F3), 2 _____ **g.** centers a page top to bottom
8. (SHIFT) - (F7), 6 _____ **h.** generates a table of contents
9. (SHIFT) - (F8), 2, 1 _____ **i.** accesses the Line Draw feature
10. (SHIFT) - (F8), 2, 6 _____ **j.** creates a second level table of contents head

Practice Exercises

1. The Steady Striders Hiking Club is creating a cover sheet mailer announcing the opening of the Upper Bumble Bee Lake trail extension from White Pine Meadows. You would like to improve the appearance of the cover sheet. To see the existing cover sheet, retrieve the file COVER.

   a. Draw a double-line rectangular box around the text in the file. Use the Erase and Move commands as needed.
   b. Enter your name and the date code on separate lines four lines below the title box.
   c. Draw a single-line rectangular box around your name and the date.
   d. Save the file as COVER.REV and print the document.

2. The file PARKS is a segment of a larger chronicle about national parks. The titles of the parks are included, but no text is in the file. You will mark and generate a table of contents of the topics in this file. Retrieve the file PARKS.

   a. Boldface and center the word "Contents." Suppress the page number on the contents page.
   b. The page numbers need to be added to the "THE NORTHWEST & ALASKA" section. Move the cursor to each page and, using the table below, add the new page number before the text.

Park	Page Number
Alaska	10
North Cascades	16
Olympic	20
Mount Rainier	23
Crater Lake	28

F6   Sh.ft F6   shift F8, Page, Suppress, this page only, F7

Sh:ft F 8 / 2 (page) / 6 (page no) / 4 (position) / F 7

use this for all the titles.

Alt F 4 using → **c.**
Alt F 5 / #1

c. Mark the titles to create a two-level table of contents. The titles that are uppercase should be level-one headings. All the other headings should be level-two headings.

Alt F5 / 5 (Define) /

d. Define a two-level, flush-right table of contents with no leaders, and position it below the title "Contents."

1 (Define Toc) / 1 (No. of levels)

e. Generate the table of contents.

f. Move the cursor to the last line in the table of contents. Insert two blank lines and add your name and the date code on separate lines.

F 7

g. Save the file as PARKS.TOC. Print the *first page* of the document only.

Alt F5 / #6 / #5 /

3. You are working on a paper for your Political Environment class and have created a draft list of the topics. You will create an outline for your paper from the topic list.

a. Using the Outline feature, create the outline displayed below:

I. Humans and Nature
   A. Population, Resources, and Pollution
      1. A Crisis of Crises
      2. Population
      3. Natural Resources
      4. Pollution
   B. Human Impact on Earth
      1. Humans in Nature: Early Hunter-Gatherers
      2. Humans in Nature: Advanced Hunter-Gatherers
      3. Humans in Nature: Agricultural and Industrial Societies
      4. Humans in Nature: A Sustainable-Earth Society

II. Environment and Society
   A. Economics and Environment
      1. Economic Growth, GNP, and the Quality of Life
      2. Dynamic Steady State and Sustainable-Earth Economic Systems
      3. Economics and Pollution Control
      4. Costs of Environmental Improvement
   B. Politics and Environment
      1. Politics and Social Change
      2. Environmental Law
      3. Long-Range Planning
      4. Cybernetic Politics
      5. Toward a Sustainable-Earth U.S. Government
      6. Toward a Sustainable-Earth World Order
   C. Environmental Ethics and Hope
      1. Hope: The People Are Stirring
      2. The Four Levels of Environmental Awareness and Action
      3. Sustainable-Earth Ethics
      4. What We Must Do: A Sustainable-Earth Program

b. Spell-check the outline.

c. Save the outline as ENVIRON. Print the file.

4. You work for the telephone company in their public relations department. For the next newsletter, you are researching communications. Retrieve the file MESSAGE. You need to add several footnotes to this document.

    a. Enter the first footnote after the comma in the second sentence of the first paragraph on Ln 1.67" Pos 4.4". The footnote is:

        Gerhard J. Hanneman and William J. McEwen, eds., *Communication and Behavior* (Reading, Mass.: Addison-Wesley, 1975), p. 85.

    b. Enter the next footnote at the end of the last sentence in the last paragraph on Ln 7.17" Pos 3". The footnote is:

        John W. Keltner, *Interpersonal Speech Communication* (Belmont, Calif.: Wadsworth, 1970), p. 107.

    c. Enter the next footnote at the end of the second to the last sentence in the last paragraph on Ln 6.67" Pos 5". The footnote is:

        Albert Mehrabian, "Communication Without Words," *Psychology Today* (Jan. 1968), pp. 52-55.

    d. Preview the footnotes. Check the footnotes for accuracy and edit them if necessary.

    e. Save the file as MESSAGE.FNT. Print the document.

WordPerfect 5.1

Glossary of Key Terms

Active printer: The selected printer used to print the document.

Address file: The secondary merge file used in a merge. It typically contains name and address data to be combined with the primary file document.

Block: A selected area of text, which can vary in size from a single character to the entire document, that is to be copied, moved, or deleted.

Boldface: Printed text that appears darker than surrounding text as a result of printing over the text several times.

Buffer file: A temporary file used to store the last three deletions made to the document.

Center: To position text in a line evenly between the margins.

Code: A hidden symbol entered in the text when a command that affects the format of the text—such as justification, margins, and boldfacing—is used.

Context sensitive: The ability of the Help system to automatically display information about the command in use.

Cursor: A flashing underscore or box that indicates where the next character you type will appear on the screen.

Default: The predefined program settings used initially by the program. Generally, these settings are the most commonly used settings.

Delete: To erase or remove a character, word, or block of text from the document.

Document: A WordPerfect file containing text and codes.

Edit: To correct or change the text or format of a document file.

Endnote: A note of reference in a document displayed at the end of the text.

Family: A section of an outline that consists of the outline level at the cursor location and any subordinates or lower levels.

Field: Each piece of data contained in a record of information in the secondary merge file for use in the merge process.

File extension: The last one to three characters of a filename following a period. Some software packages use this to identify which files were created using that package.

Filename: A unique name for identifying different documents and programs. Each filename consists of from one to eight characters, followed by a period (.) and an optional file extension.

Flush right: Positions a line of text so that the rightmost character is aligned with the right margin.

Footnote: A note of reference in a document displayed at the bottom of the page where the reference occurs.

Hard carriage return: Moves the cursor to the beginning of the next line or inserts a blank line into a text file when ⏎ is pressed.

Hard page break: A page break entered by pressing ((CTRL) - (↵)). A new page will begin following a hard page break regardless of the amount of text on the page.

Insert mode: Allows new text to be entered in a document at the cursor location by moving all existing text to the right.

Justification: When on, the text is aligned with both the left and right margins, producing even or straight margins on both the right and left sides of the document.

Leader: A series of dots or other characters between the header and the page number in the table of contents.

Level one head: The main head used in the table of contents.

Level two head: The second level head used in the table of contents.

Line: A single row of text. The WordPerfect default setting is 54 lines to a printed page.

Menu bar: The top line of the screen which, when activated by pressing (ALT) - = , displays the nine menus that can be opened.

Menu cursor: The highlight that covers the name of the selected menu.

Merge codes: WordPerfect codes entered in the primary file that control which fields are used from the secondary merge file and where they are entered in the primary file.

Mnemonic letter: The highlighted letter associated with the menu or submenu name.

Move: To remove a marked block of text from one location in a document and place it in a different location.

Newspaper columns: Columns of text that are read down the page and wrap to the top of the next column on the same page, like a newspaper.

Option: A list of command menu choices from which the user selects.

Orphan: The last line of a paragraph that is printed as the first line of a new page.

Page: The number of lines that can be printed on a single sheet of paper.

Paragraph number: The lettering/numbering system used in the Outline command to identify the topic levels and define the structure of the outline.

Parallel columns: Columns of text that are read across a page of text rather than down.

Position: The location of the cursor on a line.

Primary file: The file containing the form letter or master document that controls the merge process using merge codes.

Prompt: A question or other indication that the computer is waiting for a response from the user.

Pull-down menu: A list of commands displayed in a box below the selected menu that are available for selection.

Record: All the fields of data in the secondary merge file that may be used to complete the primary file during the merge process.

Reformat: Automatic readjustment of the text on a line after the text has been changed so that the justification is reestablished.

Repeater: The (ESC) key in WordPerfect causes a command or function to be repeated a certain number of times.

Replace: To substitute a new version of a document for the old version when saving.

Repositioning: The message displayed in WordPerfect when the cursor is directed to move to a new location.

Save: To write the current document to a diskette so that when the computer is turned off, the document will remain intact.

Scroll: To move quickly line by line, screen by screen, or page by page through the document.

Search: To move backward or forward through a document to locate a specified character string in the document.

Secondary merge file: A file used in a merge. It typically contains name and address data to be combined with the primary file document.

Soft carriage return: Carriage return entered automatically by the word wrap feature, which determines when a line of text should end.

Soft page break: A page break automatically entered by the program when the entire page is filled. The location of the page break changes automatically as text is added or deleted.

Status line: The bottom line of the screen display, which displays the document number, page, line, and position of the cursor in the document. It may also display a menu or program prompts if a command is issued.

String: A specific combination of characters and/or codes.

Submenu: Another list of commands available for selection when a command that displays a > symbol following the command name is selected.

Supplementary dictionary: A secondary dictionary used by the Speller consisting of words added by the user. Whenever the Speller does not locate the word in the main dictionary, it will check the supplemental dictionary.

Switch: To move from one document into another document file when two documents are in use at one time.

Typeover mode: Activated by pressing the (INS) key. In the typeover mode, new text replaces the existing text by typing over it.

Underline: An underscore appears under every character or space in the selected block of text.

Widow: The first line of a paragraph that is printed as the last line of a page.

Window: Division of the display screen into two parts, which allows you to view two different documents at the same time or two parts of the same document at the same time.

Word wrap: Feature that automatically determines when to begin the next line of text. The user does not press (⏎) at the end of a line unless it is the end of a paragraph or to insert a blank line.

Functional Summary of Selected WordPerfect Commands

To start WordPerfect: WP

To display Menu bar: (ALT) - =

Function	Command	Action
Cursor movement	⟶	One character right
	⟵	One character left
	↑	One line up
	↓	One line down
	(CTRL) - ⟶	One word right
	(CTRL) - ⟵	One word left
	(HOME) - ⟶ or (END)	Right end of line
	(HOME) ⟵	Left edge of screen
	(HOME) ↑ or - (minus sign)	Top of screen
	(HOME) ↓ or + (plus sign)	Bottom of screen
	(CTRL) - (HOME) ↑	Top of current page
	(CTRL) - (HOME) ↓	Bottom of current page
	(CTRL) - (HOME) page n	Top of the page n specified
	(PGUP)	Top of previous page
	(PGDN)	Top of next page
	(HOME) (HOME) ↑	Top of document
	(HOME) (HOME) ↓	Bottom of document
	(CTRL) - (HOME) ⟶	One column right
	(CTRL) - (HOME) ⟵	One column left
	(ESC) n, command	Repeat command n times
	(ESC) n, arrow	Move cursor n spaces or lines
Insert	(INS) on	Insert text
	(INS) off	Typeover text
	⟵	Insert blank line/end line
Delete	(DEL)	Delete at cursor
	(BKSP)	Delete left of cursor
	(CTRL) - (BKSP)	Delete word
	(CTRL) - (END)	Delete to end of line
	(CTRL) - (PGDN)	Delete to end of page
Retrieve	(SHIFT) - (F10) File>Retrieve	Retrieve a file
Save	(F10) File>Save>Y	Save file, resume edit
	(F7) **Y** File>Exit>Y	Save file, clear screen
Blocks	(ALT) - (F4) Edit>Block	Block on/off
	(CTRL) - (F4) Edit>Select	Move, copy, delete, or append a sentence, paragraph, page

WORD PROCESSING

Function	Command	Action
Format	`F6` Font>Appearance>Bold	Bold on/off
	`F8` Font>Appearance>Underline	Underline on/off
	`SHIFT`-`F6` Layout>Align>Center	Center text
	`ALT`-`F6` Layout>Align>Flush Right	Flush right
	`SHIFT`-`F8`, **1 7** Layout>Line>Margins	Set margins
	`SHIFT`-`F8`, **1 8** Layout>Line>Tab Set	Set tabs
	`SHIFT`-`F8`, **1 3** Layout>Line>Justification	Set justification
Print	`SHIFT`-`F7` **1** File>Print>Full Document	Print full document
	`SHIFT`-`F7` **2** File>Print>Page	Print a page
	`SHIFT`-`F7` **6** File>Print> View Document	View Document
	`SHIFT`-`F7` **S** File>Print>Select Printer	Selects printer
Outline	`SHIFT`-`F5` **4 1** Tools>Outline>On	Outline mode on
	`SHIFT`-`F5` **4 2** Tools>Outline>Off	Outline mode off
	`SHIFT`-`F5` **4 3** Tools>Outline>Move Family	Move family
	`SHIFT`-`F5` **4 4** Tools>Outline>Copy Family	Copy family
	`SHIFT`-`F5` **4 5** Tools>Outline>Delete Family	Delete family
Line Draw	`CTRL`-`F3` **2** Tools>Line Draw	Begins Line Draw
	`CTRL`-`F3` **2 1** Tools>Line Draw>1	Creates single line
	`CTRL`-`F3` **2 2** Tools>Line Draw>2	Creates double line
	`CTRL`-`F3` **2 3** Tools>Line Draw>3	Creates line of asterisks
	`CTRL`-`F3` **2 4** Tools>Line Draw>Change	Creates line of your design
	`CTRL`-`F3` **2 5** Tools>Line Draw>Erase	Erases a line
	`CTRL`-`F3` **2 6** Tools>Line Draw>Move	Moves the cursor without creating a line
Table of Contents	`ALT`-`F5` **1** Mark>Table of Contents	Marks selected text to be used in TOC
	`ALT`-`F5` **5** Mark>Define>Table of Contents	Specifies location and design for TOC

Function	Command	Action
Table of Contents (*continued*)	(ALT)-(F5) **6 5** Mark>Generate>Generate	Generates TOC Tables, Indexes, Cross-References, etc.
Footnotes	(CTRL)-(F7) **1** Layout>Footnote>Create	Allows entry of footnote references and specifies location of footnote in text
	(CTRL)-(F7) **2** Layout>Endnote>Create	Allows entry of endnote references and specifies location of endnote in text
	(CTRL)-(F7) **1 2** Layout>Footnote>Edit	Allows you to edit footnote references
Page Format	(SHIFT)-(F8) **2 6** Layout>Page>Page Numbering	Specifies placement of page numbers
	(SHIFT)-(F8) **2 8** Layout>Page>Suppress	Surpresses page numbering
	(SHIFT)-(F8) **2 1** Layout>Page>Center Page	Centers text vertically on a page
	(SHIFT)-(F8) **1 9** Layout>Line>Widow/ Orphan Protection	Turns on Widow/Orphan protection
	(SHIFT)-(F8) Edit>Protect Block	Turns on block protection for a selected block of text
Merge	(SHIFT)-(F9) **1** Tools>Merge Codes>Field	Define field names
	(SHIFT)-(F9) **2** Tools>Merge Codes> End Record	End of record
	(SHIFT)-(F9) **6** Tools>Merge Codes>More	Advanced Merge Codes
	(F9) Tools>Merge Codes> More>{End of Field}	End field
	(CTRL)-(F9) **1** Tools>Merge	Merge primary and secondary files
Columns	(ALT)-(F7) **1 3** Layout>Columns>Define	Define column settings
	(ALT)-(F7) **1 1** Layout>Columns>On	Turn on column settings
	(ALT)-(F7) **1 2** Layout>Columns>Off	Turn off column settings
Search	(F2) Search>Forward	Search forward
	(SHIFT)-(F2) Search>Backward	Search backward
	(ALT)-(F2) Search>Replace	Search and replace
Utilities	(SHIFT)-(F3) Edit>Switch Document	Switch to document 2
	(F3) Help>Help	Help

WORD PROCESSING

Function	Command	Action
Utilities (*continued*)	(F5) File>List Files	List files
	(ALT) - (F3) Edit>Reveal Codes	Reveal codes
	(F1) Edit>Undelete	Cancel/Undelete
	(CTRL) - (F3) 1 Edit>Window	Windows
	(SHIFT) - (F5) 1 Tools>Date Text	Date text
	(SHIFT) - (F5) 2 Tools>Date Code	Date as code
	(SHIFT) - (F5) 3 Tools>Date Format	Date Format
	(CTRL) - (F2) Tools>Spell	Begins Spell Checking
	(ALT) - (F1) Tools>Thesaurus	Begins Thesaurus
	(CTRL) - (F3) 3	Rewrites display of text on the screen
	(CTRL) - (↵)	Hard page break
Exit	(F7) **NY** File>Exit>N	Abandons file without saving and exits WP
	(F7) **Y Y** File>Exit **Y Y**	Saves file and exits WP

WORD PROCESSING